September–December 2022

Day by Day
with
God

Rooting women's lives in the Bible

15 The Chambers, Vineyard
Abingdon OX14 3FE
brf.org.uk

Bible Reading Fellowship is a charity (233280)
and company limited by guarantee (301324),
registered in England and Wales

ISBN 978 1 80039 133 8
All rights reserved

This edition © 2022 Bible Reading Fellowship
Cover image © iStock.com/da-kuk

Distributed in Australia by:
MediaCom Education Inc, PO Box 610, Unley, SA 5061
Tel: 1 800 811 311 | admin@mediacom.org.au

Distributed in New Zealand by:
Scripture Union Wholesale, PO Box 760, Wellington
Tel: 04 385 0421 | suwholesale@clear.net.nz

Acknowledgements
Scripture quotations marked with the following abbreviations are taken from the version
shown. Where no abbreviation is given, the quotation is taken from the same version as
the headline reference. NLT: The Holy Bible, New Living Translation, copyright © 1996,
2004, 2007, 2013. Used by permission of Tyndale House Publishers, Inc., Carol Stream,
Illinois 60188. All rights reserved. NIV: The Holy Bible, New International Version (Anglicised
edition) copyright © 1979, 1984, 2011 by Biblica. Used by permission of Hodder & Stoughton
Publishers, a Hachette UK company. All rights reserved. 'NIV' is a registered trademark of
Biblica. UK trademark number 1448790. MSG: *The Message*, copyright © 1993, 1994, 1995,
1996, 2000, 2001, 2002 by Eugene H. Peterson. Used by permission of NavPress. All rights
reserved. Represented by Tyndale House Publishers, Inc. NABRE: CEV: The Contemporary
English Version. New Testament © American Bible Society 1991, 1992, 1995. Old Testament ©
American Bible Society 1995. Anglicisations © British & Foreign Bible Society 1996. Used by
permission. NCV: NRSV: The New Revised Standard Version of the Bible, Anglicised edition,
copyright © 1989, 1995 by the Division of Christian Education of the National Council of the
Churches of Christ in the United States of America. Used by permission. All rights reserved.

A catalogue record for this book is available from the British Library

Printed and bound by Gutenberg Press, Tarxien, Malta

Day by Day
with
God

Edited by **Jackie Harris**   **September–December 2022**

Writers in this issue

Christine Platt has lived and ministered in the UK, Africa and Asia. She has written several Bible study booklets and devotional notes in multiple languages. She currently lives in New Zealand and teaches English to Asian migrants.

Rosemary Green lives in Abingdon, where her ministry as a layperson is mainly among the elderly. A grandmother and great grandmother, she has been writing for BRF for 30 years, first for *New Daylight*, and then for *Day by Day with God*.

Bridget Plass is a writer and speaker, appearing and touring with her husband Adrian all over the world. For the last ten years she has been involved in the programme at Scargill House in Yorkshire and loves living near Durham.

Rachel Turner is an author, speaker and the pioneer of Parenting for Faith. Until March 2022, she led the Parenting for Faith team at BRF, and she has worked across a variety of denominations as a children's, youth and family life pastor.

Alianore Smith is church partnerships manager for IJM UK, having previously worked for the London Institute for Contemporary Christianity (LICC). She is author of *Musings of a Clergy Child* and has been writing for BRF for four years.

Michele D. Morrison is a freelance writer, wife, mother and grandmother. She loves digging into God's word, listening for God's voice in the daily routines of life and blogging at **tearsamidthealiencorn.blogspot.com**.

Fiona Barnard is a TEFL/ESOL teacher and staff member of Friends International. She works with international students, encouraging local Christians to reach out in friendship and evangelism to make disciples. She is an honorary chaplain at the University of St Andrews, Scotland.

Helen Williams has written for BRF since 2016 but has been grateful for its work far longer. She's married to a bishop in the Anglican Church and spends time engaged in work related to this, while also working as a part-time musician.

Anne Le Tissier is an author, preacher and conference speaker, called to disciple others in their ongoing walk with God. She has been writing for *Day by Day with God* since 2005. Connect with her at **anneletissier.com**.

Revd Dr Sara Batts-Neale is a priest in the Diocese of Chelmsford. She is currently the Anglican chaplain to the University of Essex. Married to Tim, they live with a dog and host a cat.

Welcome

I always think September is a hopeful month. It has the feel of a new year as things start up again after the summer, a time for fresh starts and new beginnings. And hope is the theme that runs throughout this issue. From our opening study on how God makes everything new, through to the story of Moses, the call to persevere and on to our Advent studies of the O Antiphons and the book of Zechariah, we are reminded again and again of the hope we have in Jesus and how much God cares and provides for us.

I wonder if the O Antiphons will be new to you. I was not familiar with them, but I love the idea of Christians both past and present joining in saying these ancient words which proclaim Jesus and celebrate our hope.

We are also reminded of what God has done for us through our study on thankfulness and gratitude (starting on page 85). This is not the fashionable cure-all we often hear about, but a study of biblical gratitude. As we unpack just some of the blessings and gifts that God gives to us, our hope is renewed, and we cannot help but respond with thankfulness.

Our final study, which takes us through to Christmas and the end of the year, explores the ministry of angels. We learn how these awesome messengers prepare people to hear from God, protect them from danger, proclaim God's promises and his glory, and reassure people of his love and care.

The writer to the Hebrews exhorts us to 'hold unswervingly to the hope we profess, for he who promised is faithful' (Hebrews 10:23 NIV). Earlier, the writer describes hope as 'an anchor for the soul, firm and secure' (6:19 NIV). I like that image because it speaks of hope as something solid. It is not flimsy, wishful thinking but strong and firm, something that can hold us steady in those times when we feel anxious or overwhelmed.

As you come to these studies, may you hear hope throughout these pages. It may come in a verse, the thoughts that are shared or through the prayer or question at the end; but we pray you will hear God's word of hope for you and make that your anchor for the weeks ahead.

Jackie Harris, Editor

God is doing something new

Christine Platt writes:

Do you ever feel like you're in a rut? Is the daily grind wearing you down? Many of us yearn for something new to distract us from monotony and give us something to look forward to.

Getting something new is exciting. A new baby brings much joy to a family. A new car, a new home, even a new pair of jeans are all fun to have. God enjoys new things too. In Revelation 21:5, after explaining that there will be no more death, sorrow, crying or pain, the one sitting on the throne says: 'Look, I am making everything new!' (NLT) Everything – just imagine that!

Much of the imagery in Revelation can be hard to understand, but this chapter gives an awe-inspiring picture of heaven that awaits believers. It is a place of unparalleled beauty and wholeness, with nothing to spoil it. God was insistent that these truths should be recorded and preserved for us. He instructs the apostle John: 'Write this down, for what I tell you is trustworthy and true' (Revelation 21:5, NLT). Our all-knowing Father understood that we would need ongoing encouragement in this world with all its pain and frustration.

The insightful Russian novelist, Fyodor Dostoyevsky (1821–1881), wrote: 'To live without hope is to cease to live.' He endured seemingly hopeless situations, having been imprisoned in a Siberian labour camp for four years for his literary works (revolutionary activities), so he knew the importance of hope, and hope in Christ above all.

The sure and certain hope for believers is that there is a stunning future ahead. But maybe heaven seems a long way away when we are in the gloom of the moment. Fortunately for us impatient humans, God doesn't wait for the culmination of history to reveal this perfection, for he does new things all the time. It is part of his character and way of being.

Over these next ten days, we will look at the fresh things God does in our lives and in our world. All of these point us towards the hope of heaven where 'he will wipe every tear from their eyes, and there will be no more death or sorrow or crying or pain. All these things will be gone forever' (Revelation 21:4, NLT). Everything will be new.

The first new beginning

In the beginning God created the heavens and the earth. The earth was formless and empty, and darkness covered the deep waters… Then God said, 'Let there be light,' and there was light… Then God looked over all he had made, and he saw that it was very good! (NLT)

One day in the unfathomable mind of the Father, Son and Holy Spirit they decided to create a universe. Not just any universe, but an intricate expression of beauty and order, intended to bring pleasure to its inhabitants in the air, sea and on the land.

The Trinity were delighted with their work. They admired it from every angle and declared it to be 'very good'. They entrusted this glorious offering to humanity and for some time all went well. Everyone was happy. We rightly call it paradise. There were fruit and vegetables in abundance. No human or animal was hungry. There was peace and fulfillment in daily living. To crown it all, the divine presence was not hidden. There was a relaxed, rich relationship between the creator and all he had created.

If only it had stayed like that. We wouldn't be faced with ghastly pictures of starving children with flies crawling over their faces or crowds of refugees fleeing war and poverty, or the ever-threatening process of climate change. Our world is broken and desperately sad. The first new beginning is deeply marred.

If we struggle to cope with the pain and hopelessness surrounding us, imagine how crushingly hurtful it must be for the Holy One to witness the destruction and degradation of his beautiful ideal.

But all is not lost forever. There is still much natural beauty to admire and care for, as well as people who are made in God's image. In our own corner of the planet, we can play a part in stemming the tide of evil. Any act of kindness towards our fellow earthlings and our environment is valued and welcomed by our creator God, who, amazingly, has not abandoned us, but has a plan for humanity and the earth's renewal.

Creator God, thank you for this exquisite world you have given us and for each unique person you have put in it. Show me how to care for both the people around me and the environment, for your glory. Amen.

CHRISTINE PLATT

New mercy for each new day

'Everything I had hoped for from the Lord is lost'… Yet I still dare to hope when I remember this: The faithful love of the Lord never ends! His mercies never cease. Great is his faithfulness; his mercies begin afresh each morning. (NLT)

Jeremiah (the writer of Lamentations) is hanging on by his fingernails to his faith in God. He had just witnessed the wanton destruction of his beloved city of Jerusalem and its magnificent temple by the Babylonian army in 586BC.

Jeremiah had known something drastic was going to happen. In his prophetic book (Jeremiah), he kept calling the Jewish people to repent for their disregard of God and his holy covenant with them. He warned that the almighty would not stand idly by and let his name be dishonoured. Divine discipline was inevitable.

In the midst of the ensuing chaos, Jeremiah laments the loss of life and ongoing agony of the inhabitants of Jerusalem, and his own pain at what he has experienced. What ray of hope could there be?

Then he reminds himself of what he knows about God's character. 'His mercies begin afresh each morning.' He has not abandoned his people. Despite their constant failings there is hope for a better future.

I find it interesting that God did not come alongside Jeremiah and whisper comforting words into his ear, or even send an angel or a friend, he had to remind himself. This is a constructive example for us. When we lose sight of our Lord and Saviour and become discouraged, we need to take action and remember God's goodness and promises. The Bible is full of stories of the Lord's kindness, compassion and forgiveness. So, even if everything you hoped for from the Lord is gone, still dare to hope that you and he, together, will find a way through your present pain. With our loving heavenly Father there is always a new day with new mercy.

Write out verses 22 and 23 on a card and aim to memorise them. They will then be ready in your mind for those times when you need to be reminded to keep trusting God despite your circumstances.

CHRISTINE PLATT

New people for God's new kingdom

This means that anyone who belongs to Christ has become a new person. The old life is gone; a new life has begun! And all of this is a gift from God, who brought us back to himself through Christ. (NLT)

Scripture tells us that after creation things went badly wrong. The ground was cursed, and our first parents were ejected from the divine presence. It was clear that human beings now needed a deliverer to rescue them and guide them into new lives centred upon a restored relationship with God.

In his wondrous mercy, which we read about yesterday, God had already prepared the solution to the ghastly mess humanity had created for itself because of rebellion against him. Christ became the 'offering for our sin, so that we could be made right with God through Christ' (v. 21). There was no other way. No patch-up job or self-effort would suffice.

But, as we all experience, this 'new person' is still a work in progress. In status, believers are new people fit for God's kingdom, but, sadly, we don't always live up to that high ideal. We mess up; we doubt; we know what is right to do but somehow fail to do it. This is why yesterday's teaching, new mercy every morning, reassures us. We can confess, receive forgiveness and set out again courageously on our path of walking with God. Past sins need no longer trouble us. Sometimes it takes days, weeks, even months for that truth to sink in. Our enemy gleefully reminds us of our almost constant failures. Resist his insinuations.

This 'new person' will finally be revealed as perfect when Jesus returns. This current world is our training ground for heaven. Every time we say 'yes' to God and 'no' to Satan, our 'new person' is being formed. Paul asserts: 'I am certain that God, who began the good work within you, will continue his work until it is finally finished on the day when Christ Jesus returns' (Philippians 1:6).

My Saviour Jesus, thank you for forgiving me when I fail. I'm so grateful for your assurance that you will continue your work in me until it is finished. Hallelujah!

CHRISTINE PLATT

New bodies

We grow weary in our present bodies, and we long to put on our heavenly bodies like new clothing. For we will put on heavenly bodies; we will not be spirits without bodies. While we live in these earthly bodies, we groan and sigh. (NLT)

As the decades pass, I find myself identifying more and more with these verses. My present body grows weary, and I groan and sigh. The promise of a new body becomes increasingly beguiling.

I'm so relieved that God's plan for his people in eternity is not that we're going to be disembodied spirits wafting around. We will have new bodies which won't get tired, sick, or arthritic. Whoopee! These dying bodies of ours will be swallowed up by dynamic, indestructible life.

Having said all that, I'm enthralled by how marvellous our earthly bodies are. This hit me forcefully when I was a nursing student, and we were examining the digestive system. It's so amazingly intricate. Each section, from the mouth to the other end, is finely tuned to play its part in the digestive process. It's like a production line in a factory. Different enzymes pop up to do their thing along the way until finally all the nutrients have been efficiently extracted from our food. These nutrients then travel around the blood stream to nourish our muscles, bones and brain.

Our bodies also have incredible healing powers. I've had a few surgeries. Once the surgeon has done their work, the body takes over and eventually we're left with a neat scar.

Our response should be like that of the psalmist. 'Thank you for making me so wonderfully complex! Your workmanship is marvellous' (Psalm 139:13–15). If this is how special our mortal bodies are, how much more extraordinary our resurrection bodies will be. That is certainly something to look forward to. This hope gives perspective on those days when our bodies don't feel quite so marvellous.

How often do you thank Jesus for your marvellous body, even if it does sometimes creak and groan around the edges? Are you taking care of this incredible body he has entrusted you with?

CHRISTINE PLATT

New job

One day Ruth the Moabite said to Naomi, 'Let me go out into the harvest fields to pick up the stalks of grain left behind by anyone who is kind enough to let me do it…' As it happened, she found herself working in a field that belonged to Boaz. (NLT)

I've had several career changes throughout my working life: secretary, nurse, lecturer, speaker and writer. All these changes were daunting but ultimately so worthwhile. I was thrilled when I was asked to write notes for *Day by Day with God* in 2005. I learn so much every time I write. It's wonderful to celebrate BRF's 100 years of offering spiritual encouragement to millions. May they go from strength to strength.

The Bible gives numerous examples of people getting new jobs. Jesus' disciples went from catching fish to healing and preaching ministries. Noah went from probably a farming and business life to boat building. They showed impressive flexibility to cope with the changes life thrust upon them. Ruth was such a woman.

In Moab, Ruth's work would have been household duties, hospitality, probably being the full-time carer for her husband until he died. Her new role started with an arduous journey of 80 km, probably on foot, from Moab to Bethlehem to live among a people who were hostile to foreigners from Moab. There would not have been a joyous welcoming party for her.

Ruth didn't wait for handouts but took the initiative to go and pick up grain that the harvesters had overlooked. It was back-breaking, menial work reserved for the desperately poor. When her muscles ached and her hands were scratched and bleeding, surely she would have been tempted to moan and wish for an easier job. But she persevered through both the barley and wheat harvests.

She didn't know what the future held, but we know the end of the story. God had another change planned for her which included marriage and at least one son. She seems to have thrived in that situation as well.

Thank God that he has plans for you. They are plans for good, to give you a future and a hope (Jeremiah 29:11). Thank him for the role you have and be determined to trust him for the future.

CHRISTINE PLATT

New strength

Look up into the heavens. Who created all the stars? Because of his great power and incomparable strength, not a single one is missing... Those who trust in the Lord will find new strength. They will soar high on wings like eagles. (NLT)

I recently witnessed a lunar eclipse. The full moon was spectacular. The sky was cloudless. Clear bright moonlight poured down without hindrance. But, as the shadow of the earth spread slowly over the moon, its ability to reflect the sun's glow was blocked. The moon became reddish-brown. As a result, the stars took on a new brilliance. They were like diamonds on midnight blue velvet. Awesome.

Isaiah urges us to gaze upon and ponder the glories of nature around us to remind ourselves of how utterly magnificent God is. Faced with those dazzling stars, my earthly concerns and worries faded into their proper significance.

I think that is part of what Isaiah means when he writes, 'those who trust in the Lord will find new strength' (v. 31). Worry and anxiety sap our energy. We feel unmotivated, burdened and powerless. This is the complete opposite of God. He never gets tired and is always ready to intervene and support us. His power is limitless, and he can deal with any problem. The stars were just a sideline in his creative outburst – 'he also made the stars' (Genesis 1:16). How much more will he care for human beings whom he made in his image (Genesis 1:27)?

Focussing on the Lord's power and inexhaustible energy will plug the leak of our strength and inspiration, and channel it into praise and confidence in God's sustaining and extravagant love. We will find fresh energy to cope with whatever the day throws at us.

This morning I woke up troubled and annoyed at a situation I encountered last night. I told God how I felt and what I thought he should do about it. Today's reading has reminded me that he doesn't need my advice. He just asks me to trust him and not waste my energy sweating the small stuff.

When you're feeling weary, carefully assess your workload. Are you getting sufficient physical rest? Turn your mind to the splendour of God. Focus on the stars or the intricacies of a flower. Leave your worries with him.

CHRISTINE PLATT

A new pathway

'But forget all that – it is nothing compared to what I am going to do. For I am about to do something new. See, I have already begun! I will make a pathway through the wilderness.' (NLT)

For several years, when making trips to East Timor, we had to travel up a tortuous hill, riddled with treacherous potholes. It was only 40 km to our destination, but the journey took at least two hours. My stomach protested violently. On my last trip in 2018, I was delighted to find there was a new highway. It took a different route and was wide and smooth. Our trip was a pleasant one-hour excursion.

Through Isaiah God reminds us that when the Israelites hit an insurmountable problem, he opened up a new pathway. The crisis was a large body of water in front of them and vengeful Egyptians pursuing them. Everyone except Moses panicked. God miraculously created a dry path for his people to cross over to continue their journey to the land he had promised them. Now he says: 'Forget all that – it is nothing compared to what I am going to do.' What could be more astounding than a new dry road through a sea?

God continued to fulfil his promises and faithfully led his people through the desert and provided food and water for them. But I suggest there is also a wider meaning.

Faced with the unconquerable burden of human sinfulness, God provided an extraordinary act of mercy. In the person of Jesus, he took our sin on himself and paid the required penalty. The new pathway led to full and free forgiveness and restoration of our relationship with God. He then poured out his Holy Spirit upon all who would receive him.

Since our Lord has comprehensively dealt with these obstacles – the sea, Israel's enemies, and our sin, surely we can trust him to deal with other difficulties in our lives.

Lord Jesus, thank you for the many miracles I read about in the Bible. When I encounter problems, help me to remember that nothing is too hard for you. Amen

CHRISTINE PLATT

Change of heart

'I will give you a new heart, and I will put a new spirit in you. I will take out your stony, stubborn heart and give you a tender, responsive heart. And I will put my Spirit in you.' (NLT)

This promise of a new heart and a new spirit was given to the exiled people of Israel, yet we can also claim it for ourselves. We've already seen that when we are in Christ, we become new people. There are many examples of changed hearts in the Bible. The apostle Paul went from being a murderous enemy of Christ's followers to being their staunchest advocate. His heart and mind were completely changed by his encounter with Jesus (Acts 8–9).

I'm currently reading *Beyond the Edge: 100 stories of trusting God* by Evan Davies (CLC USA, 2012). It was written to celebrate the centenary of the mission organisation WEC. Out of the countless stories of courageous witness to unreached people groups, this one stood out.

Lily Gaynor, a British nurse, worked in Guinea-Bissau for 37 years. One night a skinny 16-year-old boy came to her house and declared, 'I want to enter God's way.' Lily warned him that he would face violent opposition from his family, but, even at his young age, he was determined to follow Christ no matter what the cost. Indeed, his relatives threatened to kill him. Paulo bravely confessed his new-found faith and told of the joy the Lord had given him. Eventually his family grudgingly accepted his decision and waited to see if the spirits of the tribe would have their revenge. Paulo stood firm and is now a pastor. His changed life had an immense effect in his village.

God can change any heart, however cynical, misguided or hostile the person may be. This spurs me on when I pray for family, friends and neighbours who seem so far from God. No one is out of reach of his long arms of love.

Thank you, Lord, that you are always looking for ways to draw more people into your family, and to give them new, tender, and responsive hearts. May my heart also be tender and responsive to your guiding hand. Amen

CHRISTINE PLATT

A new dimension of love

'So now I am giving you a new commandment: Love each other. Just as I have loved you, you should love each other. Your love for one another will prove to the world that you are my disciples.' (NLT)

Why did Jesus do such a shocking thing? He washed Judas' feet! He could have waited until Judas left on his terrible errand of conspiracy against his master and friend. But Jesus didn't. He deliberately included Judas in this overwhelming expression of love. How did Jesus feel as he carefully poured water over and dried the feet of his betrayer? How did Judas feel? Did he have even a twinge of doubt about his decision? Satan must have been astonished as well. Such an astounding act of love was beyond belief. As we now know, even that tender, compassionate, inclusive love didn't sway Judas from his treachery.

After Jesus' death and resurrection this lesson of outrageous love would have been seared into the consciences of his followers. They would have remembered every detail of that incredible evening. I can imagine them talking to each other in awed whispers: 'He actually washed Judas' feet even though he knew Judas was going to do the unthinkable.' It is one thing to serve those who love and appreciate you. It's quite another to humble yourself and be kind to those who pretend to be loyal but deceive you.

Love like that is Jesus' new commandment. It's love on a totally different level. This dimension of love proves to the world around us that we follow Christ. This is not just being nice, polite and friendly, although those things are important too. This is radical, costly love. This challenges me deeply. Do I live out anywhere near that lifestyle of love? Have I become too comfortable in my discipleship? Do I really show that depth of love to the unlovely?

Lord Jesus, thank you for loving me this much. Touch my heart to love you more. Guide me in how to love others. Help me to love in such a way that people will realise I belong to you. Amen

CHRISTINE PLATT

15

New lifestyle

Put on your new nature, and be renewed as you learn to know your Creator and become like him… Since God chose you to be the holy people he loves, you must clothe yourselves with tenderhearted mercy, kindness, humility, gentleness, and patience. (NLT)

Over these ten days we've seen that God is always doing something new. He is not content with the status quo but is constantly acting to restore what has been damaged or broken in his world.

Today's reading reveals our part in this transformative process. We are called to put off our old habits and put on new practices. The Message translation likens this to getting a whole new wardrobe. Just as we aim to dress appropriately for work, leisure or sport, so there is also suitable clothing (behaviour) for believers who are destined to live in God's kingdom.

We'd pay extra special attention to our appearance and behaviour if we were meeting the Queen. How much more effort should we take in presenting ourselves as representatives of the Lord Jesus.

I've had some falls through continuing to wear comfortable, old shoes long after the soles have worn smooth. I now have to tell myself that for my health's sake, they have to go in the bin. It's a wrench to part with them. A negative habit, like gossiping or complaining may feel comfortable because you're so used to it and everyone else is doing it. But this is not the kingdom lifestyle. We are urged to 'put to death the sinful, earthly things lurking within' (v. 5). To 'put to death' implies a deliberate decision to not allow it to resurrect its ugly head in our lives. We may need to ask others to pray with us about some of these entrenched behaviours. 'Putting to death' will not be easy.

'Putting to death' is then followed by 'putting on'. I find it a mighty challenge to remember that people around me should be able to look at my life and see the Lord's compassion, forgiveness, wisdom and love.

Choose one aspect of your lifestyle that you need to put off and one behaviour you need to put on. Make this a daily prayer. Remember God is also working in you to make this happen. You are not alone in your struggle.

CHRISTINE PLATT

How God guides us

Rosemary Green writes:

'How do I recognise God's guidance?' That often seems to be one of the trickiest aspects of our Christian lives. For some of our friends it appears so straightforward, sure of their hotline to God. I rarely find it so simple! In our readings we will think first about some of the basic principles involved, and then look at some biblical stories to see different ways in which God guided his people then and guides us now.

I wish I had space to describe the many ways in which God took my husband and me into new jobs; sometimes it was only in retrospect that we were sure we had it right. My first job offer was unsought, my 'interview' an apparently chance half-hour conversation over breakfast, with others present. God was very kind to this shy student. My well-qualified, confident fiancé however, struggled to find his first job as a curate. After some hard lessons and dead ends, he finally accepted a job that we had originally thought wouldn't fit his temperament; but the vicar mixed gentle guidance with letting Michael use his initiative – just what he needed. Next, clear that he should use his first-class theology degree for academic teaching, he applied for four jobs. Three doors closed; he accepted the fourth, training potential clergy, which combined his academic prowess with his desire to equip for ministry. We expected three to five years; it became 15 years, and he was appointed principal to use his energy and his innovative drive to move the whole college 100 miles to a new site. God often surprised us; he knew what he was doing.

We moved to a thriving student church in Oxford, to a college in Canada, back to England into a tiny team set up specially for 'the two Michaels' to boost evangelism throughout the UK; then to supposed 'retirement' – two busy, interesting, enriching and useful decades (which included work with university students in Europe, the one part of the world bypassed in the previous 60 years). Guidance came through unexpected opportunities, through consultation, through other people's initiatives, through prophetic words and pictures from friends and from strangers and through dreams. There were challenges, disappointments, setbacks, surprises and encouragements. My own ministry gifts developed – and God moulded us – wherever we moved. Through it all, I look back and thank God for leading us. We made mistakes; he never did!

Jesus sets the standard

He withdrew about a stone's throw beyond them, knelt down and prayed, 'Father, if you are willing, take this cup from me; yet not my will, but yours be done.' An angel from heaven appeared to him and strengthened him. (NIV)

Before we look at different incidents of God guiding his people, we'll think about some of the basics for discerning God's leading. If anyone knew what his Father wanted him to do, Jesus did; so we start with him.

- **His lifetime focus was to please his Father.** He told his disciples, 'My food is to do the will of him who sent me and to finish his work' (John 4:34). Obedience didn't drain Jesus; it nourished him. His life was set on discovering and doing what his Father wanted. Even in the garden of Gethsemane, aware what anguish faced him the next day, his overriding desire was, 'Not my will, but yours be done.' If we don't share Jesus' desire to obey God, we are likely to be deaf to his instructions!

- **He knew the scriptures.** At the start of his ministry, we see the devil doing his utmost to deflect Jesus from the path set for him. Jesus countered the devil's diversionary tactics repeatedly with, 'It is written'. And when the enemy cheated with a misquotation from Psalm 91, Jesus was on the ball. He knew the word of God and lived by it; so must we.

- **His life was steeped in prayer.** We are often told how Jesus went off by himself, for hours, alone with his Father. When he had an important decision to make, choosing the inner circle of his followers, he stayed up all night (Luke 6:12–13). And we are told how, after a full, demanding day (when most of us would think we deserved a lie-in!), he rose extra early to be alone with God (Mark 1:35). Cultivate a habit of quiet listening – not always chattering to God! Learning to listen in small ways will stand us in good stead when big decisions face us.

Father God, thank you that Jesus lived on earth, that he understands from the inside the ups and downs of life here. Please help me to follow his example more closely. Amen

ROSEMARY GREEN

A light for my path

Blessed are those who keep his statutes and seek him with all their heart – they do no wrong but follow his ways. You have laid down precepts that are to be fully obeyed. (NIV)

Have you ever opened your Bible at random, stuck in a pin, and expected God to guide you? Occasionally that works, though it isn't normally a reliable way of seeking his direction for life. Obedience to scripture is one of the foundations of guidance. After all, he is unlikely to lead us in ways that contradict his principles. However, rather than rely on individual verses it is better to grasp God's ways in the Bible as a whole.

So look at today's verses. Almost any section of Psalm 119 helps us to catch the psalmist's enthusiasm for God's word. He wants to learn from him and to obey him. And it's all joy (v. 14), not hard grind and gritted teeth. Notice the words 'meditate' and 'consider' (v. 15). We read for ourselves, not just rely on the preacher; we ponder; we dig deep to understand it and live it out. Our outlook is gradually moulded to match God's ways of thinking.

However, I do remember one striking occasion when God clearly spoke through one verse of scripture. Michael had promised to make a phone call one Sunday evening to accept or decline a job in Canada. It appeared to be tailor-made for him, but while his mind said yes, his heart didn't want to leave England! At the end of the evening service there was space for Spirit-inspired contributions from the congregation. A young man spoke up, with a personalised twist to Luke 9:62. Jesus said, 'No one who puts a hand to the plough and looks back is fit for service in the kingdom of God.' Michael was deeply smitten – and a complete stranger sitting next to him said, 'I don't know your situation, but I believe that word is for you.' Michael agreed – and went to make his acceptance phone call to Canada.

I was taught as a young Christian to 'hide God's word in my heart', memorising some key passages and verses. You could start today. Choose one verse from today's reading and memorise it (with chapter and verse).

ROSEMARY GREEN

A trustworthy God

Good and upright is the Lord; therefore he instructs sinners in his ways. He guides the humble in what is right and teaches them his way. All the ways of the Lord are loving and faithful toward those who keep the demands of his covenant. (NIV)

If we are going to ask God to guide our lives, we must trust him. Do we have a harsh, authoritarian god who keeps his people in subjection? Emphatically, *no*. God's promise through Jeremiah to a nation in exile was this: 'For I know the plans I have for you… plans to prosper you and not to harm you, plans to give you hope and a future' (Jeremiah 29:11). He loves us and wants the best for us.

Life was not easy for those Jews in exile. It was not easy for David who wrote this psalm. It is often not easy for us. We are in the same boat. Our desire to follow and obey him wherever he takes us is based on a relationship with a God who loves us (even when we fail him), forgives us (vv. 7, 11), teaches us (v. 12) and guides us (v. 9).

Forty years ago, I became deeply sure that our faith lies in an utterly reliable God who is good in every aspect of his being, one who makes no mistakes. One of my 'wow' moments came when the Lord used his highlighting pen on Job 42:2. After considerable pain, confusion and self-justification, Job finally stopped complaining and listened to the Lord. Job saw – and I, in my own pain and confusion, saw – that our God is 100% good and trustworthy.

So read Psalm 25 again and write down some of the phrases that speak of God's character. And what does he look for on our part? Trust (v. 2), a desire to be led and taught (vv. 4–5), confession (v. 7), humility (v. 9) are among the traits he expects. If we are flexible and open, we are more likely to be able to discover his path.

Meditate on these words of Jesus. He said, 'If you love me, keep my commands' (John 14:15). We want to find his path for us because he is a good, loving God, and we respond to his love.

ROSEMARY GREEN

God's choice

They nominated two men... Then they prayed, 'Lord, you know everyone's heart. Show us which of these two you have chosen to take over this apostolic ministry, which Judas left to go where he belongs.' Then they cast lots, and the lot fell to Matthias. (NIV)

Judas had come to a sticky end, with a sequence of greed, treachery, guilt and suicide. It seemed important to the disciples to make up the number of apostles to the twelve Jesus had appointed. (Twelve was a special number for the Jews; it signified God's power and authority; it was the age of adulthood; there were twelve tribes and twelve stones in the high priest's breastplate.) Do you share the thoughts of some who say, 'Tut-tut, weren't they relying on chance as they drew straws to determine the choice?' Think again!

First, Peter appealed to scripture (though it looks a slightly strange choice of verses!) and summed up the situation. He explained the criteria to replace the missing man; the new apostle should have long experience with Jesus and be a witness of Jesus' resurrection. Two suitable candidates, Joseph Barsabbas and Matthias, were nominated – presumably after discussion; the disciples used their minds and their first-hand knowledge. Then they prayed; they wanted God's choice and drawing lots was their way of saying to God, 'We believe you are in charge, and we want your choice.'

That is a pretty good pattern for us. They used scripture and they used their minds to see the need and who might be suitable; there was probably some 'congregational discussion'. Then they looked to God and trusted him to show his clear choice. We can do similarly; make sure that our thinking lines up with biblical thinking; use our God-given minds and our judgment to survey the situation and see what possibilities there appear to be. We can ask trusted friends for advice. Most important of all, we can come to God with open minds and ask him to show us what he wants us to do and expect him to answer. He may take us by surprise!

What decisions are you facing? You might pray like this: 'Lord, you know all the details, both now and future. Please show me what you want me to do – and may I recognise your answer, even if it is unexpected! Amen'

ROSEMARY GREEN

Setbacks and opportunities

On that day a great persecution broke out against the church in Jerusalem, and all except the apostles were scattered throughout Judea and Samaria... Those who had been scattered preached the word wherever they went. (NIV)

Tragedy had hit the church. Stephen, a man 'full of God's grace and power' (Acts 6:8), had been chosen for practical service in the food bank. But he soon showed his gifts as a preacher and healer, well-versed in scripture. His effectiveness attracted opposition, and his boldness led to death by stoning. The Christians mourned the death of this godly, gifted leader, and violent persecution followed.

But human tragedy became God's opportunity. Instead of staying clustered in Jerusalem, the persecuted Christians scattered. Rather than being silenced by fear, Stephen's example – as well as the Holy Spirit – fired them up to fulfil Jesus' words to them in Acts 1:8 before his ascension, to be his witnesses in ever-widening circles. For most of them, preaching wasn't upfront; they went round 'gossiping the gospel'. I imagine those 'ordinary' Christians chatting about Jesus to the stallholders in the marketplaces or the innkeepers where they stayed overnight. They were excited about Jesus, and they had to spill the beans! Only Philip, another of the social workers, took to the soap box.

How often God's perspective is different from ours. Stephen's death probably seemed the worst thing that could happen. But God used that event to guide them out of their comfort zone in Jerusalem to take the gospel further afield. Can you think of a time in your life when the Lord has used an apparent setback to move you in a new direction? My son and his wife, after 15 fruitful years as missionaries in Pakistan, expected to stay for another year, to advise the young Pakistani who had taken over leadership of their work. Then they heard unofficially that their visas wouldn't be renewed. If they left quickly the door would stay ajar for a possible future return; off they went to a new country.

We read in Acts 16:6–10 of another situation with many setbacks, God-given vision and a momentous advance for the gospel. Lord, help me to discern when setbacks and difficulties are your way of leading me forward. Amen
ROSEMARY GREEN

A change of direction

An angel of the Lord said to Philip, 'Go south to the road… that goes down from Jerusalem to Gaza.' So he started out, and on his way he met an Ethiopian eunuch, an important official… The Spirit told Philip, 'Go to that chariot and stay near it.' (NIV)

Excitement was high in Samaria. Philip found himself as an evangelistic preacher, with gifts of healing and deliverance (vv. 6–8). Then he had a big surprise. An angel (in what form we don't know) appeared and told him to leave his high-profile evangelistic mission and travel 50 miles or more to an unspecified spot on a desert road 70 miles long! I guess he prayed as he travelled, 'Lord, please show me why I'm making this strange journey.' So then, when he 'happened' (with God's timing) to meet the perplexed Ethiopian proselyte (a convert to Judaism), he was open to the Spirit's nudge, 'Go to that chariot.'

In his situation in Samaria, Philip needed the angel's dramatic intervention to divert him from his immediate fruitful busyness. I have never consciously met an angel, but I am convinced that they are active in the world today, God's messengers to guide and to guard us. In 2002 there was a gun attack on the missionary kids' school in Pakistan where my grandchildren were pupils. One parent saw an angel (in uniform) pointing her away from danger; two others, in white local clothes, helped a lame employee over a fence to safety before disappearing; one employee felt a hand pulling him into an empty shed; pupils in an upstairs classroom heard angels singing in the rafters.

But when already tuned-in to God, Philip didn't need such a dramatic command; 'the Spirit told Philip' to go to the chariot. We don't know how the Spirit communicated. An audible word? An inner nudge? Philip obeyed both angel and Spirit; his obedience led to the Ethiopian's conversion and baptism. The end of the story brings another unusual example of the Spirit's activity. Job done, Philip was supernaturally whisked 20 miles away and the Ethiopian continued his journey.

Think back over some of the ways God has guided you in your life, in your decision-making or your actions. List the various ways he has guided you and thank him for them.

ROSEMARY GREEN

23

An audible voice

The Lord told him, 'Go to the house of Judas on Straight Street and ask for a man from Tarsus named Saul, for he is praying. In a vision he has seen a man named Ananias come and place his hands on him to restore his sight.' (NIV)

Ananias was scared! Not surprisingly. He knew that Saul had set out from Jerusalem intent on arresting Christians, but he had not heard of Saul's encounter with the living Christ that had totally changed him. How do you think you would have responded if you had been in Ananias's shoes? He remonstrated with the Lord as he spoke to him in this vision, but the Lord's voice was clear. Ananias obeyed, and Saul's vision was healed. Ananias needed clear guidance to go into that difficult situation.

There are many occasions in the Bible when it appears that God's voice was audible, and we probably wish he would speak like that more often. But when it is needed, he does. 'John' (an alias), a vicar, was wondering whether God was calling him to a new parish. He had seen a vacancy for a role that would give him experience of being a junior member of a team leading a larger church but had rejected it as it was apparently a step down the 'promotion ladder'. But in the middle of the night he heard an audible voice telling him to apply for the post. Unlike Ananias, he didn't suspect what challenges lay ahead. He was appointed to the job and moved south with his family. Some exceedingly difficult years followed under a dysfunctional boss. But the Lord has good long-distance vision. When his boss was put aside from ministry for a serious misdemeanour, John, with his previous experience, picked up the reins in a tricky situation; acting vicar for three years while events moved sluggishly, and eventually appointed vicar. I guess there were many times during those difficult years when John wished he wasn't there. But he had the assurance of that audible voice, a special gift for special circumstances.

Lord, thank you that you know what lies ahead of us in life. Thank you that you speak to us in special ways when there are special needs. Thank you for the way you steer us through rough paths. Amen

ROSEMARY GREEN

A man who obeyed

At Caesarea there was a man named Cornelius, a centurion... He and all his family were devout and God-fearing; he gave generously to those in need and prayed to God regularly. One day at about three in the afternoon he had a vision. He distinctly saw an angel of God. (NIV)

It used to scare me that God could see the inner recesses of my mind and heart. Now it makes me feel safe, because I'm sure he loves me, whatever he sees inside. When God looked at Cornelius, he saw a man of integrity. He knew that Cornelius' prayer and generosity were a genuine expression of a good heart that was open to God. So although he was afraid and startled when he saw the angel in his shining clothes (v. 30), he was nonetheless ready to listen.

The angel's instructions were clear and specific, and Cornelius didn't hesitate. He chose three men he trusted, risking their ridicule by telling them what was happening and sent them on their way. Like the centurion who met Jesus (Matthew 8:8–9), he was an army man used to obeying and being obeyed.

What if God's instructions aren't as clear as they were to Cornelius? We can still have his attitude of obedience. 'Lord, I want to please you and obey you. I am waiting for you to show me which way to go.'

Sadly I know how painful it can be to disobey or procrastinate when God has been clear. One June, 40 years ago: 'Rosemary, that friendship is out of kilter. Put it straight.' 'Yes, Lord, I'll do that in September when things re-start after the summer.' But before the autumn, things crashed. My delay in obedience caused much unnecessary grief – but I learned an important lesson.

If God is all love, he wants the best for me. If he is all wisdom, he knows what is best for me. Well, if he both knows and wants what is best for me, what's the point of disobeying? That simple, obvious bit of reasoning has transformed my attitude to obeying God.

Lord, when you make your way plain, please help me to walk forwards, without complaint. And if the path isn't 100% clear, I'll move tentatively, asking you to stop me from making mistakes. Amen

ROSEMARY GREEN

New direction for the church

While talking with [Cornelius], Peter went inside and found a large gathering of people. He said to them: 'You are well aware that it is against our law for a Jew to associate with or visit a Gentile. But God has shown me that I should not call anyone impure or unclean.' (NIV)

God's timing is remarkable! Cornelius' envoys left Caesarea mid-afternoon and arrived in Joppa, 40 miles away, at noon the next day – just when Peter, praying on the flat roof, saw a God-given vision that he didn't like! A motley crew of animals appeared, and he was told to eat. Peter was shocked. The Old Testament forbade Jews from eating some of these creatures. The vision was repeated twice, and Peter, puzzled, realised that God meant business. Just then the strangers arrived. As they explained their errand, Peter began to understand. He invited these 'unclean' Gentiles in to eat and even to stay overnight. Next morning, he and some of the local Christians left for Caesarea.

As the story progresses, we see what a momentous change this was for the church. Jesus was not just for the Jews; he was for the whole world. They saw the Holy Spirit at work in remarkable ways in this group Cornelius had gathered. Peter and his friends became sure that Jesus was for the Gentiles as well as the Jews, and in chapter 11 we read how the Christian leaders in Jerusalem were convinced by Peter's recounting of the events. Where would you and I be without this vision and its acceptance? 'Without God and without hope in the world' (Ephesians 2:12). It needed something striking to catch Peter's attention and change his attitude.

Less far-reaching, but still important was a 'vision' for our church in Oxford. We had countless activities; leaders and members were overstretched. One woman, praying for the church, saw in her mind a potted busy Lizzie plant, weakened by its sprawling growth and needing to be pruned. As a result, we cut back some of the busyness of the church, which in turn increased our effectiveness.

Lord, thank you that sometimes you speak in dramatic ways, sometimes simply. I ask that I may be open to recognise any way you want to lead me and change me. Amen

ROSEMARY GREEN

Listening together

The apostles and elders met to consider this question. After much discussion, Peter got up and addressed them: 'Brothers, you know that some time ago God made a choice among you that the Gentiles should hear from my lips the message of the gospel and believe.' (NIV)

The believers were facing a difficult question. How much should the new Gentile believers obey traditional Jewish customs? It was tough for them, and a sharp argument started (v. 2). Remember what a huge shift there had been, even in Peter's thinking, to accept that Jesus was for the Gentiles as well as the Jews. We can learn a lot from the way they spent time discussing the questions, listening to one another and coming together to a wise decision.

So Paul and Barnabas, with some other Christians from Antioch, went to Jerusalem to meet the apostles and other church leaders. Some of the traditionalists were convinced that the Gentile believers should be circumcised (the mark of faith given by God to Abraham and his successors). First, Peter reminded his hearers how the Spirit had been given to Cornelius and others. Paul and Barnabas added their own testimony of what they had seen in their evangelistic ministry. Finally, James (Jesus' half-brother) addressed them. He appealed to scripture and suggested a good compromise, to which they all agreed, about which Old Testament laws were to be kept. I have a sense that, as he spoke, they sensed together, 'this is the right answer'.

Here are some of the guidelines they show us, whether there are corporate or individual decisions to be made. (1) It was a contentious issue, but they nipped sharp argument in the bud and went to their leaders. (2) They took their time to hear the facts, to discuss and to listen to one another. Many of our decisions need quiet, prayerful reflection and the wisdom of others. (3) They appealed to scripture. (4) They were willing to lay aside their sharply held views and to seek God's way forward. (5) They were willing to compromise. (6) They reached unanimity – and peace.

Lord, thank you for your promise to give wisdom to those who ask you (James 1:5). Please help me to discern whether other people's comments are showing me your wisdom. Amen

ROSEMARY GREEN

A new continent

During the night Paul had a vision of a man of Macedonia standing and begging him, 'Come over to Macedonia and help us.' After Paul had seen the vision, we got ready at once to leave for Macedonia, concluding that God had called us to preach the gospel to them. (NIV)

Paul and his friends had been through a perplexing time. They had tried to go into new areas of Turkey but had been obstructed. They found themselves in Troas, a port on the west coast. During the night Paul (unable to sleep or perhaps dreaming) had a clear picture of a Macedonian man, in northern Greece, pleading for help. They understood this was God's call for them to preach in Europe, and they responded immediately.

Does the word 'vision' sound somewhat daunting? You think, 'That's not for me!' But many people find a picture coming into their mind when they are praying; that seems more manageable than 'vision'. It may be a pointer from God.

During months of uncertainty before our move to Canada different prayer-pictures were significant pointers for us; they included a man standing by a plate glass mirror and a piano, and a leaping salmon! Or I think of a clergyman friend of mine with several options for his next job. 'S was the risky choice, but it seemed to fit what we were looking for,' he explained. Some friends gathered to pray. 'Our parish worker saw a picture in her mind of a long, low, stone house… My wife said it was the rectory at S.' Six months later the parish worker saw the house. 'She stood at the entrance, surveyed the long grey stone building and gasped!' That was part of the guidance that took my friend to S for 20 fruitful years.

Other friends were searching for a house near B's next job. One morning a picture of a house and garden with some key and unusual features came into B's mind, and a specific price. They scoured the area and found the house – much too expensive! But a structural survey revealed major work needed – and the property was theirs, for the price in the picture.

If such 'pictures' sound too far-fetched for you, pray that you may be open to whatever ways God wants to use to stretch your experience and to lead you on.

ROSEMARY GREEN

A God-given dream

While [Joseph] was trying to figure a way out, he had a dream. God's angel spoke in the dream: 'Joseph, son of David, don't hesitate to get married. Mary's pregnancy is Spirit-conceived. God's Holy Spirit has made her pregnant. She will bring a son to birth.' (MSG)

Joseph was perplexed! His fiancée Mary was pregnant – and he knew he was not the father. But, an honourable man, he did not want to bring her unnecessary shame. Many times in the Bible we read of God-given dreams, none more important than this one (though far-reaching, too, was Joseph's Old Testament namesake, whose gift of interpreting dreams brought him both trouble and honour – see Genesis chapters 37 and 41). Joseph was obedient to the dream, and married Mary (risking dishonour for himself, with possible accusations of a shotgun wedding). He was obedient, too, in naming the child Jesus, which means Saviour. And there were dreams to keep the infant Jesus safe from King Herod (Matthew 2:12–13).

God gave dreams to pagans as well as believers. When Nebuchadnezzar had a significant dream (Daniel 2), it was left to Daniel both to describe the dream and interpret it.

A dream was significant for us in buying a house. I first saw the bungalow on my own and went home excited by some lovely touches of relationship with the Christian owners (and I liked the house, too!) A few days later Michael came with me. While we were there, the owner told us that he had dreamt, several months earlier, that they would sell to a 'retired Anglican priest'. That fitted. Then they complained to God that he hadn't been specific enough; what about giving them a name? Their immediate thought was 'Game of Cluedo; it must be the Reverend Green'! (One of the suspects in that murder mystery board game.) That was specific! We could see that God's hand was in this, but we still took time to commit to buying it. But in the meantime, no other offers were made – and we had many happy years in that house.

God, thank you for the wide variety of ways in which you guide your people. Please help us to be sensitive, alert and obedient. Amen

ROSEMARY GREEN

Guidance for marriage

Then he prayed, 'Lord, God of my master Abraham, make me successful today… When I say to a young woman, "Please let down your jar that I may have a drink," and she says, "Drink, and I'll water your camels too"– let her be the one you have chosen for your servant Isaac.' (NIV)

For our last two readings we return to the Old Testament. The same God, before and after Christ, guides his people, both dramatically and quietly. If you have felt that some of the examples of his guidance we have read have been too 'spiritual' and out-of-the-ordinary, Abraham's senior servant (Eliezer) shows us some good guidelines for the more 'ordinary' situation.

Abraham gave Eliezer an important commission. He was to find a wife for his precious son Isaac, not from the pagan Hittites among whom he was living, but from his own relatives, about 400 miles away. That was the first guideline. Added to that, a future wife must be willing to live in the new land to which God had led Abraham.

When Eliezer arrived in the town, he used his common sense and headed for the well in the early evening, when the women would come to draw water. He was praying that God would lead him to a young woman who was helpful and generous, as characteristics of the one God had chosen. Dependence on the Lord and prayer – those are two major marks of the person who wants to go the Lord's way.

I like the gentle wisdom he showed when Rebekah appeared. First, a simple request for a drink. Then he watched, pondered, didn't rush (and continued praying, I'm sure!) before he went to the next step, asking for paid overnight accommodation. And when he discovered that she was Abraham's great-niece, that was the icing on the cake! He was quick to praise God for his leading. One question remained. Would she be willing to leave her family and travel with him? Eliezer's wise approach must have done much to reassure her that she could step into the unknown with this man.

Prayerfulness, common-sense, gentleness, wisdom and thankfulness are among the marks that Eliezer showed. Lord, please help me to develop all these traits as I seek to follow your paths. Amen

ROSEMARY GREEN

God's quiet voice

A great and powerful wind tore the mountains apart and shattered the rocks before the Lord, but the Lord was not in the wind… After the earthquake came a fire, but the Lord was not in the fire. And after the fire came a gentle whisper. (NIV)

Elijah was feeling sorry for himself. In a mighty spiritual battle, in public, the Lord had demonstrated his power over the power of the Baals. King Ahab and Queen Jezebel, furious, had threatened to kill Elijah. He ran for his life; initially 100 miles from Mount Carmel to Beersheba (two hours by car, Google tells me – but Elijah had no car!). Then another 200 miles for a month, by himself, in the desert, to Mount Horeb. He was tired, hungry, alone, scared for his life, probably in part a reaction after the spiritual 'high' on Mount Carmel. 'I am the only one left, and now they are trying to kill me too,' was his miserable complaint to God.

God graciously spoke to him, not in a powerful earthquake, wind or fire, but in a gentle whisper. Elijah listened and obeyed. We have been reading about some of the striking ways that God spoke to the early Christians, and still speaks today. He speaks too in a whisper; maybe an idea pops into my head, or it may be a gentle nudge from the Spirit. Is my 'hunch' coming from my observation or experience, or is it direct from God, or a mixture? Perhaps there is an inner sense of, 'That sits well with me' or, 'I'm really doubtful'. He uses my God-given gifts, abilities, preferences. An action isn't necessarily wrong because I want to do it!

Don't worry about stepping forward, even if you're not sure whether you have heard the whisper aright. Stay listening, go gently, not rushing, willing to admit if you've made a mistake. 'Whether you turn to the right or to the left, your ears will hear a voice behind you, saying, "This is the way; walk in it".' (Isaiah 30:21). Be encouraged. If I go wrong, he can set me straight.

Pray the Lord's Prayer: Father, may I do your will and so help your kingdom to come. Amen

ROSEMARY GREEN

Moses: a story of hope

Bridget Plass writes:

The story of Moses takes up a huge chunk of the Old Testament, beginning in Exodus 1 and finishing in Deuteronomy, as he hands over the leadership of Israel to Joshua. This is followed by his death as an exhausted old man of 120 years old. We cannot explore his career from messenger boy to commander-in-chief in depth, so I am concentrating on how, with direct guidance from God himself, Moses manages an improbable task and maintains that role for years. It is a very human story of a normal person with frailties and fears that we all experience, called to lead the greatest escape in history. There were at least 600,000 men and probably an equal number of women and children fleeing the Egyptian army, fully aware of the consequences of being caught. While easy to consign to history, as I write these words, I have imprinted on my mind TV images of thousands of terrified people in Afghanistan, so desperate to leave the country of their birth that they are risking everything in a frantic attempt to get to the airport in Kabul.

For Moses, supervising the escape was only the beginning. It was followed by the mammoth task of holding together a vast group embittered by a life of slavery and who need to learn that freedom involves responsibility. There was a lot of moaning and lack of gratitude despite God's continued support.

I am reminded of my husband and me working with young people whose lives had been extremely difficult and who struggled to cope. It was easy to become discouraged by their lack of gratitude at our attempts to improve their lives. They had been appallingly let down and it would take time and enormous patience to gain their trust and for them to make positive steps forward on their own.

We never quite lost belief in a better future for those kids, and, despite all obstacles, the saga of Moses' life is filled with hope, a hope that with God the impossible really is possible. A hope that even in the world's darkest hours unexpected change is possible. A hope that however flawed we might think ourselves, and however many times we fail, God might still have a plan for our lives which could just turn out to be far more useful than we could ever imagine. So, hope for all of us then!

Hidden figures

Now a man of the house of Levi married… and the woman… bore a son. Seeing what a fine child he was, she hid him for three months. But when she could no longer hide him, she took a papyrus basket, daubed it with bitumen and pitch, and putting the child in it, placed it among the reeds on the bank of the Nile. (NABRE)

Little baby Moses snuggled in his basket, hidden in reeds, and rescued by Pharoah's beautiful daughter is one of the most loved images appearing in children's Bible stories. Yet often missing from the story are three extraordinary women without whom God's plan would have had to take a different course. The first is, of course, his mum, whose name only ever appears in passing much later, in a list of members of the tribe of Levi: 'Amram's wife was Jochebed… To Amram she bore Aaron, Moses and their sister Miriam' (Numbers 26:59, NIV).

Oh Jochebed, what incredible courage it took to hide your baby for three months. I am reminded by my new grandson that newborns are not known for their silent submission! And you took your own life into your hands, didn't you? Dire consequences if discovered. Your final desperate act of love was to waterproof as best you could a basket that might, against all the odds, keep your precious bundle alive. But you are not alone. You had as shining examples Shiphrah and Puah, the two God-fearing midwives who, some years before, had defied the king's command to murder all Hebrew baby boys at birth, claiming that the mothers were so robust they always gave birth before they arrived, thus preventing them from carrying out their horrific designated task.

What did these three women have in common? A midwife's role is to enable life. A mother's role is to love and care for her children. All three risked their lives because they refused to go against who they were designed to be. God must have been very proud of them. Incidentally, it is worth remembering Aaron, three years older, who only escaped the cut because of the midwives' determination. And without Aaron?…

Dear Father, please help me to find the courage to bravely fulfil whatever role has been given to me. Amen

BRIDGET PLASS

Who am I?

After Moses had grown up… he saw an Egyptian striking a Hebrew… he struck down the Egyptian and hid him in the sand. The next day… two Hebrews were fighting!… 'Are you thinking of killing me as you killed the Egyptian?'… Moses became afraid… fled from Pharaoh and went to the land of Midian. There he sat down by a well. (NABRE)

Never has there been a time in the UK when identity has been such a big issue. Ethnic background, cultural norms and gender diversity have become increasingly pertinent to discern who you are and to give you a sense of value. I have often wondered what it must have been like for Moses: growing up in the palace, educated in Egyptian, wearing their clothes, eating their food; but isolated, aware that his family and his tribe worshipped a different God, were subjected to daily abuse and had none of the luxuries afforded to him. Was he pointed at in the street as the only Hebrew boy of his actual age in existence? It was going to blow one day and when he sees yet another of his fellow men abused, he simply can't stand it any longer.

His immediate need to cover up what he has done shows his awareness that, as the unwelcome adoptee in the family of a brutal dictator, his position was extremely precarious. It is hard to imagine how devastated he must have been when he discovered his action hadn't endeared him to his fellow Hebrews, and that he was in even greater danger. He didn't belong anywhere or to anyone. What must he have been feeling as he sat by that well, homeless and tribeless?

Maybe we would find the answer if we really listened to one of the many displaced people who risk everything to escape the threat of death, but find themselves aliens in a foreign land, belonging nowhere and to no-one.

It is so easy for us to judge behaviour that may seem reckless or wrong without really understanding the reasons. Maybe today is a good time to listen.

BRIDGET PLASS

The gap years

The priest of Midian had seven daughters, and they came to draw water… [for] their father's flock. But shepherds came and drove them away. So Moses rose up in their defence… the man gave Moses his daughter Zipporah in marriage. She conceived and bore a son… Gershom, for he said, 'I am a stranger residing in a foreign land'… Moses was tending the flock of his father-in-law Jethro, the priest of Midian. Leading the flock beyond the wilderness, he came to the Mountain of God, Horeb. (NABRE)

We learn at the end of Exodus 2 that the king has died, so presumably Moses could have safely returned to Egypt. However, God has other plans for him. Having heard the cries of his people and feeling very sorry for them, God needs to prepare their future leader. The time for the Israelites' prayers to be answered is not yet right.

Back to Moses sitting hopelessly by the well in Midian and we discover he is still the same impulsive character we met in Egypt. He didn't think of the consequences of killing the Egyptian which landed him in a mess, and he doesn't think of the consequences now, but this time it brings him acceptance into a new family, a new identity and a new future. God gives Moses a sabbatical from all the pressure he has had to cope with so far – some gap years, a wife and son, and time to enjoy his new family far away from all the pressures of the jarring factions of his former life.

I confess to often feeling frustrated with God that he doesn't do what I want him to when it seems obvious to me that it needs doing right now! Here I can see that the journey out of Egypt has already begun, in the inner building of his chosen leader's core strength through love, acceptance, physical activity and time. But, as we are about to discover, the job has only just begun. It is a great relief to me – and maybe to you – that impulsiveness and failure don't seem to count us out when it comes to being used by God, even if we are not (thankfully) going to be given a mammoth task like Moses!

How many times do we feel frustrated that what we can see as clearly needing to happen doesn't despite all our prayers? Maybe today we can try to trust a little longer that God has heard us.

BRIDGET PLASS

Mission Impossible

When the Lord saw Moses coming near the bush… he called him by name… Moses answered, 'Here I am'. God replied, 'Don't come any closer. Take off your sandals – the ground where you are standing is holy. I am the God who was worshipped by your ancestors' (CEV)

And so it begins! A burning bush that does not burn. A voice calling him by name. It belongs to God himself, so holy and powerful that he warns Moses the very ground is sacred. Let's not minimise the impact. Jehovah himself, after years of absolute silence, is talking to Moses from inside a bush about a future too wonderful to contemplate. A future Moses is not only going to be involved in but is apparently going to lead.

'Off you pop,' says God. 'Go to the king and tell him what's to happen.' Moses must have wondered if God knew him at all – a murderer so cowardly he hid his victim in the sand and then ran away. Even after being told exactly what to say to the leaders of Israel and witnessing a snappy miracle or two – a walking stick that turns into a snake, a hand that turns leprous and then heals – Moses still stubbornly argues his case that he is not the man for the job: 'I've never been any good at speaking and I can never think of what to say.' God says he'll give him the script, but still Moses begs him to send someone else. Finally, God says he can take Aaron with him. This is the beginning of many such exchanges between Moses and God in which Jehovah, the great I Am, God of Abraham, Isaac and Jacob, like many a parent before and since, appears to get worn down by the persistence, passion and dare I say stubbornness of his child and caves in.

Dear Father God, you know us: all our past mistakes, all our future fears. Help us to say yes to your plans for us despite what we think of ourselves. Amen
BRIDGET PLASS

Small change in his pocket

Moses and Aaron went to the king of Egypt… the king gave orders to his slave bosses… 'Don't give the slaves any more straw to put in their bricks. Force them to find their own straw wherever they can, but they must make the same number of bricks as before'… The men knew they were in deep trouble… [and] went to see Moses and Aaron… 'We hope the Lord will punish both of you for making the king and his officials hate us.' (CEV)

Having persuaded the leaders of the tribes of Israel that God is going to mastermind their escape from Egypt things don't start well. The first attempt to persuade Pharoah to let the people go results not only in a refusal but also in things getting much, much worse for the Israelite slaves. No wonder they turn on Moses and Aaron. So much for words and miracles – what counts is what is happening now!

But just look how Moses' relationship with God is changing. He is no longer lost for words and doesn't hold back. 'What is going on God? Things are getting worse not better. If the Israelites won't listen why should the king of Egypt? You haven't done a thing to help and I'm getting it in the neck as always.' Well he didn't quite say that, but there is no doubt that his newly found slim confidence is dented. So what is going on? Maybe Moses needs to learn a crucial lesson. That for a while at least, his role, with Aaron, is to buckle down and accept they are merely 'postmen' delivering messages. The rest will be up to God.

John Wimber once said: 'I'm just loose change in God's pocket, he gets to spend me as he chooses.' Maybe Moses is beginning to understand the value of this and even to want to be used in this way. Personally, I have come to love the idea that even if I am only small change, if I give God what I am, he can use me to make a small positive difference to someone or to a situation.

Thank you, Father God, for allowing me to jingle in your pocket. Help me to want to be used in whatever way you want. Amen

BRIDGET PLASS

On that night

'On that same night I will pass through Egypt and strike down every
firstborn of both people and animals. I am the Lord. The blood will be a
sign… when I see the blood, I will pass over you… for the generations
to come you shall celebrate it as a festival to the Lord,' (NIV)

While Egypt is reeling under the stubbornness of Pharoah and the famous
nightmare plagues which followed each refusal to let God's people go free,
we see some important, if subtle, changes in the mindset of Moses. He
moves from fear of Pharoah to blazing anger. His final exchange with the
king sees him storming out of the room in disgust. More importantly, he
moves from fear of God to something more allied to a partnership and to
an unwavering, absolute trust. He has no doubts about what God is capable of, but he is now aware of just how far God is prepared to go to fulfil
his promise to free Israel, his chosen nation. This close relationship is vital
if, together, they are going to keep the unruly tribe of Israel – all 600,000 of
them plus women and children – intact once they are free.

First, Moses must persuade his fellow Hebrews to prepare very specifically for a ritual involving the blood of a lamb. This will not only ensure
their safety when the angel of death passes over their houses but will also
become a regular opportunity in the future to remember what God did for
them that night. The ritual of Passover is celebrated by Jews to this day
throughout the world.

Many years after Moses, Jesus longed to share the celebration with his
friends. It was during the Passover meal that he asked them to remember
him, as alone he prepared to take the place of that sacrificial lamb. Why?
Because that is how far the Son of God was prepared to go to rescue us. Not
just an empty ritual then or now, Passover still symbolises the love of God
that has never changed. So, it was a rather important job for 'postman'
Moses to pass those instructions on!

---

*Dear Jesus, thank you for leaving us with a tangible way to remember you,
lest we forget your love for us that took you to the cross. Amen*
BRIDGET PLASS

It's not fair

When the Israelites saw the king coming with his army… they also complained to Moses, 'Wasn't there enough room in Egypt to bury us? Is that why you brought us out here to die?'… Moses answered… 'The Lord will fight for you'… The Lord said to Moses, 'Why do you keep calling out to me for help? Tell the Israelites to move forward.' (CEV)

This a pattern that is going to be repeated again and again throughout the 40 years the children of Israel trail miserably through the desert before reaching Canaan. Whether it's facing the impassable Red Sea, finding the only water they have available is bitter, running out of food or meeting enemy armies, the pattern is the same. The Israelites get frightened or hungry or grumpy (often I might say with good reason), and moan to Moses who moans to God or pleads with him depending on the circumstances, and God throws it back in Moses' court or gives in after Moses pleads the people's cause. Sound familiar? Whether globally or even in our own family, when life becomes intolerable and we feel incapable of moving forward, we tend to get angry and blame those who we feel are responsible.

I take huge comfort in the fact that God always listens to Moses however fed up he might be. Sometimes he throws the ball back into Moses' court: 'You know what to do.'

After her young husband died, a close friend of ours went up on to the hills near her home and screamed out to God. She was hurt and angry, but she knew where to take all her pain – she took it all to the Father she knew could cope with it, the Father Jesus tells us hears our cries. And sometimes we know deep down that it's up to us either to sort ourselves out or to step up to offer whatever we can. Maybe that's why God gives the Israelites such detailed laws. Sometimes however, we may need to seek appropriate help – a lesson Moses is also going to have to learn.

Father God, please help us to look carefully at exactly what we should do. Leave it to you? Seek help? Face up? Amen

BRIDGET PLASS

Home truths from Jethro

'Listen now to me and I will give you some advice, and may God be with you. You must be the people's representative before God... But select capable men from all the people... let them serve as judges for the people at all times, but let them bring every difficult case to you.' (NIV)

The arrival of Jethro, Zipporah and the kids after such a long separation is perhaps something we can all relate to since the family separations during pandemic lockdowns. What a joy it must have been to have his family there – the people who knew him as Moses – son-in-law, shepherd, husband and dad, and who aren't part of the whole Exodus story. What a reunion meal it must have been. What long chats by firelight as Moses fills Jethro in on all that has happened. Next morning Jethro is able to watch Moses in action, as from morning to evening he witnesses Moses dealing with endless disputes, reminding people of the laws God has given and making final decisions.

Perhaps Moses hoped for a pat on the back, but that is not always what family is for, is it? How often have we heard the words: 'you are wearing yourself out,' 'working too hard,' 'need to delegate'? This is exactly what Moses hears now and maybe God has already prepared him so he can actually listen to the older man's advice. In recent memory hadn't Moses had to accept physical help from Aaron and Hur to keep his arms aloft so that Joshua could triumph in battle against the Amalekites? Just the sort of visual aid God might use to plant a seed in his leader's head and, as it so often is with those who become famous, just the sort of family pressure needed to keep Moses' feet on the ground. Moses agrees to delegate all but the most serious cases to men chosen for their capability and honesty.

Jethro's advice reminds us that we are designed to be team members. Sharing responsibilities can be tricky, especially if it seems easier to just get the job done ourselves, but let's make sure we give others a chance to be involved.
BRIDGET PLASS

The 'Dictaphone' years

On the morning of the third day… Mount Sinai was covered with smoke, because the Lord descended on it in fire. The smoke billowed up… and the whole mountain trembled violently. As the sound of the trumpet grew louder and louder, Moses spoke, and the voice of God answered him. (NIV)

And here begins a new chapter in the story of Moses. He's going to have to listen extremely carefully to this explosion of power and might, so terrifying that the very earth trembles. This is a stern God promoting zero tolerance for misbehaviour and demanding fair settlement in disputes in order to help Moses govern an ever expanding and increasingly disparate mob, and also to set out standards for future generations.

The closest I can get is an experienced head teacher brought in to steer an unruly school: jumping on the slightest deviation from correct uniform, setting high standards, encouraging progress and praising good behaviour. As well as the ten crucial commandments in Exodus 20, there are innumerable detailed laws dictated by a concerned God acutely aware of every aspect of day-to-day living. Massive prizes for good behaviour include reinforcing the original promise to get them safely to the promised land and the offer of a very special relationship. 'Now if you obey me fully and keep my covenant, then out of all nations you will be my treasured possession' (v. 5). But it all has to be passed on word for word and there is a great deal of it. A man purportedly poor at public speaking is having to learn fast on the job. In the process he discovers he is becoming a protective buffer between the Israelite leaders and their terrifying God. They plead with Moses, 'Speak to us yourself and we will listen. But do not let God speak to us or we will die' (Exodus 20:19).

Exodus is a fascinating read but I'm glad our buffer is now Jesus, the great high priest, understanding our temptations and problems and reducing the laws into two all-encompassing and positive challenges: Love God with all your heart and love your neighbour as yourself (Matthew 22:36–40).

Oh Jesus, you knew just how hard your apparently simple commands would be for us. All our heart? Love God? Love our neighbour? Do we love God and others enough? Help us to sift our thoughts today. Amen

BRIDGET PLASS

Master architect

'Tell everyone in Israel who wants to give gifts that they must bring them to you'… Suddenly the sacred tent was covered by a thick cloud and filled with the glory of the Lord. And so, Moses could not enter the tent. Whenever the cloud moved from the tent, the people would break camp and follow. (CEV)

God is on a roll. Having set out a law structure designed to keep his chosen people healthy, safe and orderly, and to endeavour to keep them focussed and faithful; he then sets Moses a new challenge. Moses is to project manage the building of a tabernacle specifically designed in incredible detail by God himself. It is to be a home fit for a king – the king, God himself – so he could travel with his chosen people and also act as a focus for worship for the people. Thank goodness Moses had learned to delegate!

This is one of the most positive periods for the Israelites. For a start they actually had something to do and were able to employ skills they may have thought they had left behind in Egypt. The sacred furniture, the priestly garments and fittings were to be elaborate and made to an exact design. Spiced anointing oil and incense were to add fragrance, and carved lampstands to give light. Perhaps the most significant thing for those involved was that instead of demanding their involvement, God actually asked the Israelites of their own free will to donate materials and offer their skilled labour. For once there was a sense of harmony. Admittedly Moses had been away from the main body of travellers for over a month, but he's feeling refreshed and positive, and probably pleased with life and hopeful for the future as he comes down the mountain with two plaques engraved with the commandments by God's own hand.

Dear God, thank you for this reminder that you never bully us into working for you but let us join in. Amen

BRIDGET PLASS

Trouble in the family

After the people saw that Moses had been on the mountain for a long time, they went to Aaron and said, 'Make us an image of a god who will lead and protect us. Moses brought us out of Egypt, but nobody knows what has happened to him.' (CEV)

What is it about coming down from a mountain top experience with God (or even going away on a much-needed holiday) that so often ends in disappointment? Maybe the expression 'having your head in the clouds' has something to do with it. Admittedly communication was limited, but there is no doubt that Aaron, Moses' right-hand man from the beginning, felt resentful that he had been left behind for so long to manage the complaining, bored Israelites. They wanted a god they could see. He succumbed to their demands and organised the making of a golden bull, agreeing they could have a festival to worship the god Baal.

What must Moses have felt, after leaving the sanctuary of being in the cloud of the presence of God, when he heard the wild drunken chanting followed by Aaron's feeble excuse that when gold earrings were thrown into the fire they magically turned into a golden bull. Actually, we know what he felt: furious. He smashes the tablets of stone, a personal gift from God to the camp, grinds the gold into powder, mixes it with water and makes the Israelites drink it. Mind you, his anger was nothing compared to God's, whose response was to destroy the lot of them. But Moses, once described as the humblest man who ever lived, offers to take the blame even if it means he himself is destroyed. We all get disheartened when, however much we hope God has changed us, the same old faults seem to rear their ugly heads whenever we are under pressure. Let's take heart from the changes that have taken place in Moses. The same man who ran away from Egypt, and who begged God to find someone else to face Pharoah, is standing before God and bravely offering himself as a sacrifice.

Dear Father, maybe today is the day for us to thank you for the positive changes we discover in ourselves, and to let others know we see the changes in them. Amen

BRIDGET PLASS

43

The special relationship

Moses used to set up a tent far from camp. He called it the 'meeting tent', and whoever needed some message from the Lord would go there… Everyone would… watch him enter. Then they would bow down because a thick cloud would come down in front of the tent, and the Lord would speak to Moses face to face, just like a friend. (CEV)

We hear a lot about special relationships between countries but know that they can falter and fail all too easily. Despite many times when this could have happened, the relationship between God and Moses just gets stronger the longer they journey together. God appears to love the way Moses takes him on, pleading the cause of the Israelites not once but many times. He trusts Moses to carry out his wishes and even considers him a friend.

You might think that in asking God if he can see him Moses has over-stepped the boundary, but God is open to considering it – although it was going to have to be carefully stage-managed to prevent Moses being destroyed by the force of God's power. God hides in the cleft of a rock and Moses is allowed to catch a glimpse of his back. He then spends more time on God's mountain cutting new tablets of stone and, as he returns, his face is so radiant he has to wear a veil. God's glory has literally rubbed off on him!

While I have never met anyone who has had to wear a veil to protect me, I have met a few people who almost visibly glow. Men and women who have spent so much quality time with their maker that the presence of God within them is almost visible.

Jesus tells us to go into our room and shut the door and talk to our Father. Not just as a discipline, but in order to get closer to him – and maybe we too will grow shinier with time!

BRIDGET PLASS

The finishing line

'The Lord is slow to anger, abounding in love and forgiving sin and rebellion. Yet he does not leave the guilty unpunished.' (NIV)...
[Moses] said, 'Look, you rebellious people, and you will see water flow from this rock!' He raised his stick in the air and struck the rock two times. (CEV)

The closer the end was in sight the worse things got for Moses. We are even told he expressed the wish that he could die! Finally, however, the grumbling multitude arrive at Paran, a few days' march from Canaan, and young men from each tribe are sent to spy out the land. All but two return afraid and demoralised, convinced there was no way they could defeat the giant-sized occupiers. The camps are plunged into disarray as the Israelites bewail their certain fate. Only Joshua and Caleb argue God will be on their side. God arrives and is so furious he threatens to destroy everything and make a new nation from Moses. Once again, we are reminded of the unique relationship Moses has with God, as he begs him to change his mind, actually having the audacity to remind Jehovah himself that he is slow to anger! Coming from Moses this is a bit rich, as we shall see.

God agrees to refrain from wiping out his chosen nation and to continue the journey with them. But more enemies need defeating: internal rebellions flare, idolatrous behaviour needs stamping out and moaning never stops. Moses is getting tired and old, and perhaps this explains why Moses lets his temper get the better of him. Instead of speaking to the rock as God has commanded, he strikes it twice. Water flows out, but unfortunately so do all Moses' hopes of crossing the border into Canaan. But why such a dire consequence? Maybe because, for whatever reason, Moses is no longer listening closely to God's detailed instructions. Maybe he thinks he knows the pattern – always before he's been asked to use his stick! Such lapses could endanger their safe passage into Canaan. After so many exhausting years the role of leader passes to Joshua, and Moses' job is finally over.

We all know how easy it is to think we know exactly what God would do and stop listening. Let's take time today to turn up our spiritual hearing aids.

BRIDGET PLASS

The Moses interview

'You are the Lord God, and you know what is in everyone's heart. So I ask you to appoint a leader for Israel'... The Lord answered, 'Joshua son of Nun can do the job. Place your hands on him to show that he is the one to take your place'. (CEV)

Well, Moses, would you like to talk us through your life so far?
'Well, as you know, I grew up in the Egyptian palace, then after killing someone and running away (not proud of it), I spent 40 peaceful years looking after sheep. I met my wife, had our first child and it was a nice exist-ence until God spoke to me from a bush! Bit of a shock being asked to tell Pharoah to let the Israelites leave Egypt, I can tell you. Turned out to be a bit of a challenge as you may have heard but, of course, God was operation commander as he has been throughout the years which followed.

'I'm not going to pretend it was an easy ride. I spent a disproportionate amount of time trying to keep folk fed and watered and trying to keep us moving forward, and occasionally I did get a bit fed up – well actually I lost my rag on more than one occasion. Mind you, so did God! I had more than a few tricky conversations persuading him to stay with us.

'Highlights? Lots, of course: walking through the Red Sea, getting the tabernacle built, surviving battles, passing on the commandments and especially talking face-to-face, well face-to-back anyway, with God.'
So, did Canaan live up to its milk and honey reputation?
'Ah well, can't say really, didn't quite make it, same old temper got me into trouble again – should have known. You see, I could talk to God about anything – even take him on – as long as I followed orders. Truth be told part of me was relieved to be able to pass the leadership on to Joshua. I was pretty creaky by then. Great fellow. Lots of energy and a good head on his shoulders. He's going to need it.'

Well maybe all we can say is, 'Thank you, Moses.' His was a life lived to the full – sometimes shining, sometimes not, but hanging on in and never giving up. An encouragement to all of us.

BRIDGET PLASS

The way to blessing (Romans 12)

Rachel Turner writes:

At first glance Romans 12 can appear to be a list of commands for Christians to achieve in their daily lives: be living sacrifices, use your gifts, love people, bless those that curse you. On and on it seems to go, a list of impossible standards to strive for in daily Christian life.

I read it a bit differently. In this passage I see a blessing, a deep and powerful invitation to live in a freedom that we didn't have before Jesus. Paul is writing to small house churches in Rome, in the midst of persecution and struggle. He helps them see how different life can be when we live as God has called us to.

If we could truly live the way Paul writes in Romans 12, we would be living an organic, authentic life before God, alongside a community of people who love and sacrifice for each other. We would feel hopeful and needed, loved and cared for and effective in ministry. We would be filled with peace and love in all circumstances and be passionate about our faith – even in the face of evil.

This passage isn't a list of dreary rules to march along to. This passage is outlining the way to flourish with God and with each other, because Jesus gave us access to him and his Holy Spirit who lives in us.

It may take some honest looking at ourselves to face these truths that Paul shows us. Not because changing our behaviour is hard (which it is), but because of what that behaviour shows us about our heart, our insecurity, our anger, our lack of generosity or our fear of losing something. Romans 12 can challenge us deeply. Sometimes I can only read one sentence before I think, 'Okay, I need to wrestle with how I feel about that.' You may even want to disagree a few times; I know I did. There is blessing in the wrestling, because when we wrestle, we are engaging. When we engage, then we are allowing ourselves to be transformed.

I need to be transformed because I want to be the person who instinctively and wholeheartedly lives like Jesus did. I want to be a part of that Christ-like community who loves and perseveres well and shares the good news of Jesus with others.

May God bless each of us as we open ourselves to this transformation this week.

Lifesong

So brothers and sisters, since God has shown us great mercy, I beg you to offer your lives as a living sacrifice to him. Your offering must be only for God and pleasing to him, which is the spiritual way for you to worship. (NCV)

The early Christians in Rome were very familiar with the idea of bringing sacrifices to gods. Around Rome there were multiple temples to worship a variety of gods and the pagan people would attempt to gain the favour of these gods by bringing them sacrifices. Some sacrifices were animals to be killed, others included wine, perfume or food. People tried to please their gods with sacrifices that were costly to them.

Paul wanted the Christian Romans to know how to please the one true God. Not with physical sacrifices to be brought, but with an entire life given over to God.

The band Casting Crowns has a song called 'Lifesong'. The premise is that how we live our lives is somehow woven into a worship song for God. I love the idea that every thought I have, every choice I make, every time I love or put others first, every moment I am grateful to God, or manage to bite my tongue, all somehow becomes a song of worship to God.

My song may sound like a child learning an instrument – sometimes filled with terrible notes, awkward pauses and unsuccessful attempts at melodies. I am still learning how to make my entire life a beautiful song, but one thing it will be, is authentic.

Every day, moment by moment, we can choose to worship God with our lives. And as our loving Father, he will delight in such worship as we give what we have to him.

God, I want to worship you with my life, to be a living sacrifice for you. Be my companion in my days. I give you what I am now, imperfect and sincere. Thank you for loving me. Amen

RACHEL TURNER

A new way of being

Do not be shaped by this world; instead be changed within by a new way of thinking. Then you will be able to decide what God wants for you; you will know what is good and pleasing to him and what is perfect. (NCV)

I have lived in the UK for 20 years now. When I first moved here, I felt lost. Everything felt different. In my old home, I could navigate conversations and develop relationships automatically. But once I moved to the UK, I didn't know how to make deep friendships or even how to make an acceptable cup of tea for guests. My old way of thinking didn't work anymore.

When I read this passage, I am struck by how, as Christians, we have to go on a journey of transformation. Our instincts, our past, the way we have been shaped for so long now needs to change. In Christ, we are new creations and we need to be transformed into a whole new way of thinking. This transformation is not a one-off moment. It is a daily journey of shedding what was before and learning the new.

It took me ages to learn how to make a proper cup of tea and start a queue at a bus stop. I had to miss the sun enough that I learned to race outside when the sun shone and anticipate the glory of June strawberries. After 20 years I'm still learning.

As we walk with God, we can ask him to help us change the way we think. His word challenges and shapes us. The time we spend with him in prayer and worship softens and grows us. He guides us into new truths and invites us into better ways of living. We are on a journey of transformation. What takes conscious effort now, will become instinctive thoughts and behaviours tomorrow. Each new way of thinking enables us to grow in confidence in our ability to know what God is asking in each moment.

God, help us to learn what parts of our old way of thinking need to be transformed into your way. Show us how to learn your new ways, that they may become our new natural instincts. Amen

RACHEL TURNER

Embrace the puzzle life

Each one of us has a body with many parts, and these parts all have different uses. In the same way, we are many, but in Christ we are all one body. Each one is a part of that body, and each part belongs to all the other parts. (NCV)

Many of us want to be good at everything. Maybe that's not quite true. Maybe we just feel like we *should* be good at everything. We *should* be great at administration, hospitality, leadership, communication, teaching, serving, loving, helping the poor, encouraging and anything else we can think of.

We can feel ashamed when we realise we aren't able to do it all. Every weakness we have can feel like a failing – a place where we should be succeeding and yet are not good enough to do it.

But in this passage Paul tells us that we are lying to ourselves. We were never meant to be great at everything. We were designed to have weaknesses and strengths. Our weaknesses are a strategic choice by God to leave space for other people in our lives. To leave space for us to be alongside others in theirs. They are designed for us to experience the utter joy of being part of the body of Christ.

We are a puzzle piece, designed to lock into others to create a strong, useful body. And yet we spend a lot of our time trying to make ourselves square and complete, all on our own.

What would it look like if we began to accept and be grateful for our weaknesses because they create opportunities for others in our lives? What would it be like to think, 'How can I help this person in their weakness' rather than be angry at their imperfection?

God is still growing and changing us. Our weakness today may be our strength in ten years' time. May we be graceful with ourselves and others, reaching out in each other's weaknesses and calling for each other's strengths in our lives.

God, bring me peace about my weaknesses. Thank you for making us to fit together, for calling us to be part of each other within the body of Christ. Help me find those who need me and who I need in my life. Amen

RACHEL TURNER

Navel gazing

We all have different gifts, each of which came because of the grace God gave us. (NCV)

Many of us love categorising ourselves. In magazines and online we are offered light-hearted quizzes to help us find out what old movie character we are most like. At work we are often offered more practical analysis to explore what our 'Myers-Briggs' type is or what 'colour' we are in our professional lives. We love finding out what category we fit into.

I often find that this passage in Romans leads us to the same kind of scrutiny of ourselves. What gift do I have? What label should I put on myself? Am I a teacher? A server? What box should I put myself in?

But Paul was encouraging a group of Christians to bring the fullness of themselves to the community they were placed in. He didn't want them worrying about being the whole package. He wanted them to be their piece, in whatever came natural to them. I don't think he meant us to attempt to narrow ourselves into one box. Too often we feel trapped into only serving in the area we have experience in.

We are all more than one thing. Our gifts may not be limited to our skills. We may be a teacher in our day-to-day life, but we may also have a gift of hospitality. We may be able to play a musical instrument, but we may also have the gift of encouragement.

Let's not waste time trying to put ourselves in a box or trying to articulate what we think our gift is. Our goal is to give ourselves freely.

Let's learn to ask, 'What needs do I see in front of me that I feel drawn to help with?' Let's ask God, 'Where do you want me to serve?'

God, show me where I can be of the most use. Free me from any box I am clinging to. Show me how to be my part of the whole picture, where I am right now, without worry or labels. Amen

RACHEL TURNER

Not just a performance

Love must be sincere. (NIV)

There are many times I wince at scripture. When the truth it speaks gets around my defences and pokes me straight in the heart. This verse is one of them.

Love must be *sincere*. Not a performance. Not merely an action. Love must be true, real and authentic. When I read in scripture that God loves us, I really believe it. I believe in the deep, sincere, love of God that he feels when he looks at me. I trust in it. I count on it. I don't think he is merely being nice to me or tolerating my presence and calling it love. I believe he really loves us all.

Jesus specifically calls us to love our neighbours, to love our enemies, to love our brothers and sisters in the faith. What if he really means *love*… in the way he loves us? How often is the love that I give to my family, my friends, my colleagues, my community simply a performance of love rather than actual love? How many times have I simply been kind or polite to someone and checked it off the Christian requirement of being loving?

If we were to truly love, we would have to change our hearts, not just our behaviour. We would have to ask ourselves, 'How can I see others the way God sees them?' If we were to sincerely love, we would need to work hard to root out in our hearts any bitterness, anger or fear in how we think about others, so love could grow. If we were to genuinely love, we would need to face our own reactions and wonder, 'What is happening inside of me that is stopping me from loving this person sincerely?'

It's a beautiful call to love. It's a crucial call to love. Because being sincerely loved can transform people's lives. Being free to sincerely love transforms us, too.

God, open the eyes of my heart to who I have not been sincerely loving. Take me on a journey of learning how to cultivate a heart of love for that person. Teach me how to love like you, Jesus. Amen

RACHEL TURNER

Above yourselves

Love each other like brothers and sisters. Give each other more honour than you want for yourselves. (NCV)

The call to love echoes throughout scripture. I love the mutuality of it. You love me, and I love you. We love God, and he loves us.

Sometimes, though, I think we keep an internal tally to make sure that it doesn't get unbalanced. I invite you over to my house, you invite me over to yours. I babysit your kids, you return the favour. It is all nice and even, and we feel safe in that equality. But there are times when we need to know that it is okay to accept love and help when we cannot possibly return it.

I have recently been through a season where I needed help. I needed grace. I needed others to love me and seek me out; to forgive me when I couldn't live up to what I wanted to do and hoped I could do and love me through it. I can never repay the love that has been poured out on me in this season. In the same way, I can never repay the love God has for me. It is generous and uneven, and I am grateful.

There will be times in all of our lives when we need to rest in the love of others, as they love and care for us, with no expectation or possibility of repayment. One day, someone may need you to love them in that way, and you may be able to step into that gap. But if you can't right now, that is okay. Part of being a Christian is allowing others to love you with the love of God, to accept that others are choosing to put you above themselves because they feel called to and to simply accept their beautiful gift with gratefulness.

God, help me rest in your love. Thank you for calling your people to love sacrificially and sincerely. Help me accept it when I need it, and love others when they cannot return it. Amen.

RACHEL TURNER

As far as it depends on you

If it is possible, as far as it depends on you, live at peace with everyone. (NIV)

Paul often makes me smile. He seems so rooted in the reality of life. He knew better than to simply tell us to live at peace with everyone. Some people make that impossible for all sorts of reasons. Paul doesn't let us off the hook though. He doesn't say, 'Some people are just evil and impossible, don't even try.' He calls us to be peace-bringers, even in the midst of relationships that are hard. Even when those we are in relationships with are wrong. Even when evil has been done to us. We are called to peace.

My sense of injustice rises up against that idea. I want God's justice to be done, I want evil to cease. I want to make it happen!

God very clearly assures us that he will avenge those wrongs, but he is equally clear that our part is not going to be armoured up next to him, riding into the battle to bring pain and vengeance to the evil doers. Our job is in loving our enemies and seeking peace where we can. Riding into battle sounds much easier.

Bringing peace requires me to try to walk with love and integrity as defined by God, not by me or anyone else. It demands that I hold myself to the standard of Jesus' love for his persecutors as he was being crucified. It calls me to pray for those doing evil around me like Stephen did when he was stoned; to have compassion on our jailers like Paul did when he was in prison.

Paul did not say that we had to achieve peace with all around us, just that we were to do all we could to bring it, in a way that honours God.

God, I trust your justice. Fill me with your peace that surpasses all understanding, and your love for all humanity, so I can do all that I can to seek peace with those around me. Amen

RACHEL TURNER

Meeting Jesus

Alianore Smith writes:

When you think of Jesus, what comes to mind? Do you think of what he's done – crucified, buried, risen, ascended? Do you think of him in purely theological terms – the second person of the Trinity, uncreated and eternal? Do you think of how he has been presented to you by other people? When you think of the person of Jesus, do you tense up, or do you relax? Do you expect rebuke or welcome?

Over the next fortnight, we're going to be exploring the person of Jesus through the eyes of those who met him. From crowds to Pharisees to outcasts, we shall learn about his character and his attitude towards us.

As we begin this journey, however, I want us to pause and notice something: of the 14 people we will meet who encounter Jesus, we know the names of only four of them. What does this tell us? Many things – but one I want to draw out: we do not need to be famous, powerful, or well-known to meet with Jesus. All we need is a willingness to approach him.

When Jesus describes himself in Matthew 11, he simply says this: 'I am gentle and lowly in heart' (Matthew 11:29, ESV), and that description comes with an invitation: 'Come to me… and I will give you rest' (11:28).

We will discover many things about Jesus over the coming weeks: his compassion, his power, his kindness, his anger at injustice, and his self-proclaimed mission on earth. But we would do well not to forget that when he speaks of his heart, Jesus proclaims himself as gentle and lowly.* What an approachable Saviour. What a glorious, generous friend. And although we explore history in the gospels, we are reminded in Hebrews 13:8 of this simple truth: 'Jesus Christ is the same yesterday and today and forever.'

And so, as we journey together in getting to know Jesus more in the coming weeks, I pray that you would find in him what you need – for his yoke is easy and his burden is light.

May you find rest for your soul and peace for your troubled mind. May you leave knowing and loving Jesus more.

*I took this point from and have been particularly blessed by Dane Ortland's book *Gentle and Lowly: The heart of Christ for sinners and sufferers* (Crossway, 2020), which I would thoroughly recommend.

The temple crowd

Then he [Jesus] rolled up the scroll, gave it back to the attendant and sat down. The eyes of everyone in the synagogue were fastened on him. He began by saying to them, 'Today this scripture is fulfilled in your hearing.' All spoke well of him and were amazed at the gracious words that came from his lips. 'Isn't this Joseph's son?' they asked. (NIV)

When you meet someone new, how do you introduce yourself? Or perhaps for a professional bio – what do you say? For work, you probably give some of your qualifications and credentials, information about your family, and then a fun fact to make you seem relatable and cool. In social gatherings, it's probably your name and how you're connected to the group.

What we have in this passage is Jesus' bio – his first introduction of himself in public. He's just been baptised and then led by the Spirit into the wilderness for 40 days, tempted by the devil, and then has 'returned to Galilee in the power of the Spirit'. He's been teaching in synagogues and now he's in his hometown. Back where he grew up – where people remember his first steps.

This is Jesus' reintroduction into society, his introduction to the world. And how does he decide to introduce himself? With the words of the prophet Isaiah. We learn so much about Jesus from this introduction. He is anointed by the Spirit of the Lord. He will be proclaiming good news to the poor. He cares about freedom, about healing, about the end of oppression. He is announcing the year of the Lord's favour.

But here's what fascinates me about these verses: the words he reads (vv. 18–19) are *just the beginning of what he preaches that day*. He rolls up the scroll, sits down, and then – as everyone's attention is on him – *begins* by saying 'today this scripture is fulfilled in your hearing.' These words – these powerful, prophetic, mic-drop words – are just the beginning.

Jesus introduces himself to us. Today, as then, he invites us to get to know him more.

Consider what you know about Jesus – what more do you want to learn? What is there left to discover? Ask God to teach you more about himself in the coming weeks as we journey through this study together.

ALIANORE SMITH

The Samaritan woman

The Samaritan woman said to him, 'You are a Jew, and I am a Samaritan woman. How can you ask me for a drink?' (For Jews do not associate with Samaritans.) (NIV)

Let's take a moment to talk about Jews and Samaritans. A lot of us will be familiar with the story of the Good Samaritan, and this has similar vibes. The religious differences between Jews and Samaritans were serious and deep-rooted. They were not to be sniffed at. This wasn't just a cool kid associating with a nerd – this was Jesus risking ritual defilement by asking to share a water vessel.

Add in the fact that this was a Samaritan *woman*, and you begin to understand why she was quite so surprised that a Jew such as Jesus would speak with her, let alone ask her for a favour.

There are reams upon reams of sermon material in these 30 verses – living water, Jesus' divine knowledge, the treatment of women and understanding of marriage in ancient culture… all are rich and ripe for learning. But today, let us consider what we learn about Jesus from this woman's interaction with him.

We learn immediately – even before his incredible knowledge and his cryptic reflections about living water – that he is not afraid of ritual defilement. He is not ashamed to be seen with a Samaritan. With a Samaritan woman. With a Samaritan woman who has been ostracised by her community, forced to collect water at the hottest part of that day, mistreated by men and all but cast aside by those around her.

Jesus is not afraid of who society, culture or law says we are. He is not put off by our worthiness, our cleanliness, our holiness – or lack thereof. Jesus is for everyone – he is cool water on a hot day, a well that never runs dry. Like this woman, we may not understand it – but that doesn't mean we don't need it.

Father, thank you that you are for everyone – regardless of status or reputation. Please remind me of this both for myself and for those who I sometimes wish to write off. Thank you that you welcome all with open arms. Amen
ALIANORE SMITH

The bleeding woman

Then the woman, knowing what had happened to her, came and fell at his feet and, trembling with fear, told him the whole truth. He said to her, 'Daughter, your faith has healed you. Go in peace and be freed from your suffering.' (NIV)

This scene opens with Jesus powerwalking through a crowd. He's following Jairus, a synagogue leader, who has asked him to come and heal his dying daughter. Amidst this crowd is a bleeding woman; she's been that way for twelve years. She is desperate for healing.

Jesus the healer is in town – but he is powerwalking. He is surrounded. He is on a time-critical mission to save a dying girl. The woman is at the end of herself, confronted with a clearly busy Jesus who is helping someone who wouldn't even touch her because of her uncleanliness – what would you do?

This woman fights through the crowd, touches the hem of Jesus' garment and is healed. Mission accomplished.

But Jesus stops. Abruptly, he turns. Time is of the essence, but someone has reached out in faith to touch him – and he wants to know who. There is something here about Jesus' priorities. He could have been content with knowing that *someone* has been healed, but instead he seeks out a personal interaction.

Even when it appears that he is on a mission, that he is bound up with something else, that there is another, needier, more urgent case for him to attend to, what we learn is this: Jesus is not afraid of being interrupted.

He is not inconvenienced by our requests. But he is also not some kind of healing jukebox – he is a healer who longs for a personal interaction, who looks for our faith, who calls us 'daughter' and who seeks out of the clamouring crowd those who have come to him. Even when he's powerwalking. Even when time is of the essence.

No one is too insignificant for Jesus. No interruption is inconvenient. For he longs for a personal interaction with those who reach out to him.

Do you ever find yourself thinking that Jesus is too busy for you? That anything you bring to him is an inconvenient interruption from his 'real', more important work? Spend some time reflecting on and praying about this today.
ALIANORE SMITH

The Centurion

When Jesus heard this, he was amazed and said to those following him, 'Truly I tell you, I have not found anyone in Israel with such great faith.' (NIV)

When was the last time you stood up for or represented someone in front of someone else? Maybe getting in the middle of a fight, perhaps on behalf of a colleague in the face of unfair demands, or in writing a reference for a friend.

Unless you're a barrister, it's unlikely that you spend a great deal of time interceding – bridging a gap between two parties, advocating for others – in your daily life.

This story, however, is an example of intercession: a centurion's servant is paralysed and suffering greatly. The centurion – a non-Israelite – makes his way to Jesus and requests that Jesus remotely heal his servant, declaring that he is not worthy to have Jesus in his house. And Jesus does just that – he commends the centurion's faith, and he heals his servant from afar.

What we learn from this passage is that Jesus answers petitions made by those with faith on behalf of those who have none – on behalf of those who cannot speak for themselves.

There is power in intercession. The centurion in this passage physically goes into Jesus' presence, but his servant remains far away. Yet still the servant is healed. Today, we cannot physically go into Jesus' presence, however we can approach him through prayer.

There is power in intercessory prayer – in 'standing in the gap' for people as you pray for their healing, their salvation, their blessing. Colossians 4 instructs us to 'continue steadfastly in prayer', James 5 says the prayer of a righteous person is powerful and effective.

The well-loved hymn 'What a friend we have in Jesus' puts it like this: 'Have we trials and temptations? Is there trouble anywhere? We should never be discouraged, take it to the Lord in prayer.'

How can you intercede for others today? Make a short list of people to bring before Jesus and request healing, salvation, or blessing on their behalf. Commit to praying through your list daily in the next week.

ALIANORE SMITH

59

The widow of Nain

Soon afterward, Jesus went to a town called Nain, and his disciples and a large crowd went along with him. As he approached the town gate, a dead person was being carried out – the only son of his mother, and she was a widow. And a large crowd from the town was with her. When the Lord saw her, his heart went out to her and he said, 'Don't cry.' (NIV)

Can you remember the worst day of your life so far? A shock diagnosis, the death of a loved one, a traumatic event... in our broken world there are plenty of contenders for such a title.

In this story, we join a woman on the worst day of her life so far. She'd thought it was bad when her husband died, but now her only son – her sole hope of provision – is gone too.

The community has gathered to mourn with her as the body is carried to the burial plot – most likely where the boy's father was also buried. I guess she had hoped she wouldn't live to see another such journey.

But here she is again. The worst day of her life.

Suddenly, some strangers appear. A group of men, led by Jesus. Jesus sees her. He is moved by her circumstances. He approaches. And he does the unthinkable: he touches the body. He makes himself unclean. And then he speaks: 'Don't cry'. He speaks again: 'Get up!' And the dead boy rises. Hope rises. And suddenly, it's not the worst day of her life anymore.

What do we learn about Jesus from this interaction? Many things – his power to raise the dead, his willingness to become unclean. But perhaps what we learn most about is his compassion: 'When the Lord saw her, his heart went out to her' (v. 13).

Deaths weren't unusual in Jesus' world. Funerals were regular occurrences. But for some reason, in this situation, Jesus steps in. Right into the middle of this widow's worst day. He sees, he feels, he approaches, he touches, he speaks. And suddenly, hope rises. May he do the same for us today.

Father God, even in my worst day, would you be close – would you see, feel, approach, touch, speak and heal. May hope rise – even in the darkest of nights. Amen

ALIANORE SMITH

The boy who gave his lunch

'Here is a boy with five small barley loaves and two small fish, but how far will they go among so many?' (NIV)

This story is told time and again in sermons and children's talks – lauded as a great example of giving what you have to God and seeing it multiplied. And yet, we know very little about this boy. We don't know if he volunteered his lunch, or whether the disciples just happened to spot him sitting down and pulling it out of his knapsack.

We don't know how he felt about his lunch being used in that way. We don't know if his lunch was precious to him – perhaps the only meal he was going to get that day. We don't know what his parents sacrificed in order to provide him with five small loaves and two small fish. We don't know what he was thinking as Jesus took it, blessed it and shared it around.

We don't even know the boy's name. We do not hear him speak, and we are not privy to his reaction when his packed lunch is suddenly used to feed this 'great crowd'. We do not know how he explained to his family what happened.

Put yourself in the boy's shoes for a minute – how would you feel? What would you be thinking? What would you want to say?

We learn plenty about Jesus from this passage: with him, there is always enough. He is a miracle worker and a provider.

But what do we also learn about Jesus from his unspoken, unwritten interaction with this small boy? I think we learn that he doesn't write anyone off. Children with their lunchboxes have just as much to offer the kingdom of God as anyone else. Jesus sees as much potential in a child clutching his tuna sandwiches as he does in a disciple sitting at his feet. What a gift.

Father, thank you that you see potential in all of us, and that in the kingdom of God no-one is written off. Please remind me of that when I am close to dismissing my or others' contributions. Amen

ALIANORE SMITH

The woman caught in adultery

Jesus straightened up and asked her, 'Woman, where are they? Has no one condemned you?' 'No one, sir,' she said. 'Then neither do I condemn you,' Jesus declared. 'Go now and leave your life of sin.' (NIV)

What is something that really, really annoys you? Perhaps it's trivial like loud eaters or slow walkers. Or perhaps it's more serious, like liars or cheats. What we discover in this passage is that hypocrisy is something that really annoys Jesus. The Pharisees present him with a woman caught in adultery and ask a trick question: 'Do you think we should stone her?'

If he says no, he's saying that people don't have to follow part of the Mosaic law. If he says yes… well, it's obvious what that would mean.

I wonder how this woman felt as Jesus paused and wrote on the ground. She was waiting for a verdict from him – her life was in his hands. She was probably afraid of what he was going to say, possibly frustrated at his prolonged silence. The Pharisees certainly were – pestering him with questions until his anger erupts: 'If you're going to hold her to these stand-ards', he says, 'be sure to hold yourself to them too.'

Jesus has turned the Pharisees' words back on themselves. He hates hypocrisy. He has no time for those who will happily point out the sin of others, clamouring for them to be punished, whilst refusing to engage with their own.

Jesus' words to the Pharisees are clear. And they are clear to us also: don't hold others to standards you wouldn't hold yourself to. We might get angry at slow walkers, but when we're dawdling along looking at our phone, we don't really care about our pace. We might hate liars, but when we tell small untruths we can quickly come up with reasons why it was okay *this time*.

Jesus hates hypocrisy, but – and we see it with this woman – he does not condemn those who come to him in sorrow for their sins.

May we remember that today.

Are there times when you hold others to a higher standard than you hold yourself? Why is that? Take some time to bring your hypocrisy before God and ask for his forgiveness.

ALIANORE SMITH

Lazarus

The dead man came out, his hands and feet wrapped with strips of linen, and a cloth around his face. Jesus said to them, 'Take off the grave clothes and let him go.' (NIV)

If you're anything like me, you don't know what it's like to die. Therefore, it's reasonable to conclude that we may need to use our imaginations a little more than usual for today's study.

In the first verse of this passage, we read that Lazarus is sick. We don't know what kind of sick, and we don't know how sick. All we know is that he is sick – and sick enough for his sisters to tell Jesus about it.

And then we know that Lazarus dies. We don't know if it was prolonged and painful, or the kind of death that comes all at once. We don't know if he was scared, or peaceful, or oblivious. All we know is that he died.

And then, the next time we see Lazarus – previously sick, now four-days-dead – he is walking out of his tomb; hands and feet bound and blinded by a cloth around his face.

I wonder how Lazarus experienced this course of events. Was he cross with Jesus as he died, in the same way his sisters were? Did he have hope until the very last moment that Jesus would show up and heal him? As he took his final breath, could he have even begun to imagine that, actually, it wasn't to be his last act on earth?

I think what we learn about Jesus from this passage is quite simple, and also remarkably complicated: Jesus is surprising. He doesn't do what we expect him to do when we expect him to do it. Invariably, he does something better when we're pretty sure it's already too late.

If you're anything like me, that's not the Jesus you want a lot of the time.

But if you're anything like me, it's almost certainly the Jesus you need.

Where do you feel that Jesus is dragging his heels, not showing up where and when you need him to? Listen to the song 'You Came (Lazarus)' by Bethel Music and bring before God the miracles that you need from him today.

ALIANORE SMITH

Martha and Mary

'Lord,' Martha said to Jesus, 'if you had been here, my brother would not have died. But I know that even now God will give you whatever you ask.'… When Mary reached the place where Jesus was and saw him, she fell at his feet and said, 'Lord, if you had been here, my brother would not have died.' (NIV)

Today, we're embracing the beauty and majesty of scripture by looking at the same story from a different person's perspective. God's word is like a many-sided diamond – from every angle you get a new perspective, a renewed sense of the beauty.

I find Martha and Mary's bluntness refreshing. For both of them, their opening words to Jesus are simple but devastating: 'if you had been here, my brother would not have died'. I wonder how Jesus felt as these words were said to him the first time. He does not seem troubled as he speaks with Martha in verses 21–28: 'Your brother will rise again.'

But when Mary comes to him with the same accusation – accompanied this time with tears – Jesus is 'deeply moved in spirit and troubled'. And Jesus weeps. The only other time we see Jesus crying in the gospels is over the city of Jerusalem in Luke 19. Jesus weeping is a rare and holy thing.

I wonder how Mary and Martha felt, seeing that their words had brought Jesus to tears. Maybe they felt justified in their anger. Perhaps they felt guilty. Perhaps they were glad of the solidarity of his tears amidst their own grief. Perhaps it was a mix of all those and more because feelings are rarely one-dimensional.

What do we learn about Jesus from this passage? I think we learn that he loved. He loved Lazarus, and he loved Mary and Martha. He joined them in their grief – and he mourned with them as they mourned. Even though he undoubtedly knew what was to come next, at that moment, love looked like weeping.

And so Jesus wept. And Jesus loved. As he still does for us today.

Are your prayers ever as blunt as Mary and Martha's conversation with Jesus? What's your 'if you… then…' with God right now? Bring it to him in prayer and ask him to show you his love in the midst of it.

ALIANORE SMITH

The woman who anoints

A woman in that town who lived a sinful life learned that Jesus was eating at the Pharisee's house, so she came there with an alabaster jar of perfume. As she stood behind him at his feet weeping, she began to wet his feet with her tears. Then she wiped them with her hair, kissed them and poured perfume on them. (NIV)

When did you last ugly cry? That kind of face blotchy, snot smeary, wailing crying that you can't stop. What was the reason?

Today, we meet a woman who is ugly crying. Our passage uses the word 'weep', which feels far more delicate and sanitised than what she was probably actually doing. When you weep, you do not produce enough tears to wet someone's feet. That only happens when you ugly cry.

Why is she ugly crying? Jesus tells us – 'her many sins have been forgiven'. She is overwhelmed by the kindness, grace and forgiveness of Jesus.

Have you ever ugly cried over the goodness of the gospel? Have you considered your sin, and considered God's grace that covers it? 'Whoever has been forgiven little loves little'. The flip side of this is that whoever has been forgiven a lot loves a lot: as we see in this woman.

If you're really, truly, deeply honest with yourself, how much have you been forgiven? A little? Or a lot? How do you feel about Jesus in light of that?

Today, we learn that Jesus is kind. We learn that Jesus offers forgiveness in the face of our sins. Jesus' grace is deeper than our deepest shame.

So today, do not be afraid to acknowledge the depth of your sin: the brokenness you carry, the perfectionism that burdens, the harsh words, the cruel actions, the unkind thoughts. Consider the way it weighs heavy upon you, like a backpack too large for a small child.

And then consider that Jesus has taken it away. Gone. He has replaced it with kindness. Grace. Forgiveness. A lightness you could never achieve on your own.

And if you find yourself ugly crying? That's okay too.

Thank you, Jesus, that your grace runs deeper than my deepest shame. Thank you that you're not afraid of my ugly cries. May I never lose the wonder of the forgiveness you offer. Amen

ALIANORE SMITH

Pilate's wife

While Pilate was sitting on the judge's seat, his wife sent him this message: 'Don't have anything to do with that innocent man, for I have suffered a great deal today in a dream because of him.' (NIV)

Do you remember your dreams? Whether stress related, cheese-induced, or just the result of an overactive imagination, those of us who remember our dreams can likely name a few that have stuck with us through the years.

This mention of Pilate's wife and her dream is just one verse in the midst of a highly charged scene. It feels like an aside, easy to skip over, a bit like a dream that only remains in your mind for your first waking moments and then is forgotten in the busyness of the day.

But God doesn't waste words – every sentence of scripture is 'God-breathed and useful for teaching, rebuking, correcting, and training in righteousness' (2 Timothy 3:16). So, what's going on here?

I wonder whether Pilate's wife usually remembered her dreams. I wonder what it was about this dream – which caused her to 'suffer a great deal' – that convinced her to contact her husband and declare Jesus to be innocent. How did she even know who Jesus was? How did she know her husband would be involved in his trial that day? How did she know he was innocent?!

This passage shows us that Jesus can appear in dreams. That he can communicate to people through their dreams, can reveal truths about himself to individuals as they sleep. And it's not just limited to the gospels: today, thousands of people – and particularly Muslim-background believers – credit a dream of Jesus as a key moment in their conversion to Christianity. Nabeel Qureshi, author of *Seeking Allah, Finding Jesus*, is one such believer.

Jesus is passionate about people coming to him – even those who have never met a Christian in their lives, or whose countries are closed to Christianity. And he will work through a myriad of ways to draw us to himself. Dreams are just one of them.

Today, consider praying for those in countries closed to Christianity, that Jesus would introduce himself to people in dreams and visions. Check out the charity Open Doors for more resources.

ALIANORE SMITH

Barabbas

Now it was the governor's custom at the festival to release a prisoner chosen by the crowd. At that time they had a well-known prisoner whose name was Jesus Barabbas. (NIV)

'I volunteer as tribute!' That's the memorable line spoken by Katniss Everdeen in *The Hunger Games*, as she offers herself up in place of her sister, who's been chosen for a fight-to-the-death competition. It's a goose-bump inducing scene, in both the book and the film.

Katniss' sister is innocent. She's young. She's helpless. Katniss comes in as an older sibling to rescue and protect her, and the readers completely understand. In her situation, they would probably do the same.

Not so in this passage. Barabbas was not innocent. He was the archetypal Jewish rebel – the modern-day equivalent would probably be some kind of political fanatic, hell-bent on fighting violence with violence in order to win power.

I wonder how Barabbas felt in this moment of sudden freedom. We do not know if he was stood in front of the crowd, hearing them clamour for his freedom, or if he was in his prison cell and suddenly, unexpectedly released. We don't know if Barabbas knew that his life was traded for another's. But Jesus knew.

Jesus was innocent. Jesus had been handed over to Pilate out of the chief priests' and elders' self-interest (v. 18). Jesus was not a violent revolutionary – he brought peace and healing and good news. But despite this, the crowd call for his death – and Pilate allows it. Jesus, the innocent, takes the place of the guilty.

The thing is, we are all Barabbas. Whether we are stood in front of a crowd or trapped in a cell of our own making, waiting to hear of our punishment, we are all Barabbas. We are all sinful, broken and despairing.

Jesus is innocent. But he stands in our place. Takes the punishment we deserve. He volunteers as tribute. When Jesus dies, we go free.

Thank you, Father, that Jesus died in my place. Thank you that he volunteered as tribute, even though I don't deserve it. Thank you that because of his death, I go free. Amen

ALIANORE SMITH

The centurion at the cross

With a loud cry, Jesus breathed his last. The curtain of the temple was torn in two from top to bottom. And when the centurion, who stood there in front of Jesus, saw how he died, he said, 'Surely this man was the Son of God!' (NIV)

When was the last time you had an 'aha!' moment? An epiphany if you will. A moment where, suddenly, something clicks into place in your brain, and you see things in a new light.

What we witness in this passage is an 'aha!' moment. An epiphany from one of the centurions overseeing Jesus' execution. We don't know what role he would have played before this moment – was he the one holding the nails as they went into Jesus' hands? Were they his muscles that held Jesus down? Did he help pull the cross upright with Jesus hanging off it? What had he already seen? What did he think of this so-called 'King of the Jews' whose death he had been instructed to oversee?

We do not know much about this centurion. Jesus doesn't even appear to address him directly. But he watches events unfold – the mocking of the crowd, the conversation with the rebels on either side, the all-encompassing darkness that falls in the middle of the day, Jesus' loud cry of God-forsakenness. He's seen it all.

And now, with Jesus' last breath, the curtain of the temple is torn in two and the centurion has an epiphany. Something clicks into place: 'Surely this man was the Son of God!'

We do not know what happens to the centurion after this. Perhaps he thinks his revelation comes a moment too late: Jesus is dead. End of story. We don't know if, three days later, he hears stories of Jesus' resurrection. We don't know if he became part of the early church, an evangelist about this Jesus of Nazareth, Son of God.

But we know this: when confronted with the reality of the crucifixion, he proclaimed the truth about Jesus. Will we do the same?

Consider the events of this passage. Imagine yourself in the scene, as the centurion was. What is your response? How will this impact your life moving forward?

ALIANORE SMITH

Thomas

Then he said to Thomas, 'Put your finger here; see my hands. Reach out your hand and put it into my side. Stop doubting and believe.' Thomas said to him, 'My Lord and my God!' (NIV)

Are you ever tempted to gloss over your doubt to be accepted into the faith community? Do you consider your doubt shameful? That it means you're not a good Christian? Do you sometimes wonder if God is angry at your doubt? I know I do.

Today, let's think about doubt. So, what's your biggest doubt about Christianity? Creation out of nothing? The virgin birth? The inerrancy of scripture? Jesus' death? Jesus' bodily resurrection? Whether prayer works? Whether God is truly good? Take a moment to name it. Don't be ashamed. You're certainly not alone.

I love that God was kind enough to include this passage about Thomas in the Bible. Thomas is – as so many of the disciples were – incredibly human. But he's also incredibly honest. When presented with his grief-stricken friends proclaiming they've seen their dead leader alive again, he's understandably sceptical.

What I like about Thomas is that he's honest about his doubt. He doesn't try to hide it. He doesn't try to blend in with the crowd. He doesn't want to be accepted so much that he lies about where he's at with his faith.

And this passage shows us that Jesus isn't put off by our doubts. In fact, he walks right towards them. He confronts them head on. Thomas sets the parameters of what he needs to believe, and Jesus offers them to him.

And then – I love this – Thomas makes a declaration: 'My Lord and my God!' This is the first time in John's gospel that anyone has directly referred to Jesus as God. Out of doubt comes fresh revelation. New insight and deep wonder are birthed from honest questions and blunt scepticism.

Jesus can do the same with our doubts today.

Consider the doubt that you named at the beginning of this study. Bring it to Jesus in prayer – even if you're not sure he's listening. Name it, explain it, and then ask God to give you a fresh revelation of himself despite it.

ALIANORE SMITH

Keep on keeping on

Michele D. Morrison writes:

In this, BRF's centenary year and my tenth year in the stable of BRF writers, it seems appropriate to be looking at the subject of perseverance, or stick-to-it-iveness, as my mother always called it. Congratulations to BRF for staying the course, which has no doubt included many challenges demanding stick-to-it-iveness.

A few years ago, my husband and I attempted the pilgrim route to Santiago de Compostela. We bought the right gear, read a few books, packed our backpacks and set off by train from Aberdeen. Arriving in Saint-Jean-Pied-de-Port, we collected pilgrim passes and slept that night; then, after a good breakfast, we were off to conquer the Pyrenees. A painful 27 km later we – or rather I – limped in agony into a crowded Roncesvalles, where we struggled to find beds for the night. My poor knees gave out on the Pyrenees and we had to postpone our pilgrimage.

How many of us embark on the way of faith only to give up at the first hurdle, owing to painful events, inadequate preparation, or distractions?

Eugene Petersen coined an apt definition of perseverance in the title of one of his books, *A Long Obedience in the Same Direction*. It is a book on discipleship, and what is discipleship if not a calling to persevere in faith, following Jesus? Jesus is always on the move and disciples need to keep up.

And where does he lead? He calls each of us to a unique path which, in my experience, often descends into challenging circumstances which really test our mettle. As we persevere in faith, one step at a time, hand in hand with our Saviour, we are purified just like gold is tempered in the fire.

The word perseverance carries a connotation of dogged determination. There's no hint of joy or fulfilment. But the way of Jesus is upside down. The heart surrendered to God is lit up by his inspiration and love and filled with a quiet joy.

The joy of the Lord is your strength, the Bible says. Joy is found in persevering faith.

Over the next fortnight, we will look at some of the shining examples of perseverance in the Bible, exploring priorities and attitudes, so that in our twilight years we can say, as Paul did, 'I have fought the good fight.'

Perfect perseverance

'My soul is crushed with grief to the point of death.'... 'My Father! If it is possible, let this cup of suffering be taken away from me. Yet I want your will to be done, not mine.' (NLT)

The Saviour of the world was perhaps never more human than when he confessed to his three closest friends that his soul was crushed with grief. It may seem astonishing that, hearing such a heart-felt cry of anguish, his best friends just fell asleep. But his best friends didn't have an answer. Jesus knew they didn't have the answer; he knew his Father alone had the answer, but he craved prayer support, feeling wobbly in the face of what he knew was coming.

Jesus is the picture of perfect perseverance. Faced with more than he could humanly bear, he turned to the source of all help. He hoped – he prayed – to be let off the hook, to be reprieved from the torture to come. But in a staggering act of love – for us, for the world, and for the Father – Jesus continued to seek and be fully surrendered to his Father's will. What a Saviour!

How did he do it? We are given pictures throughout the gospels of Jesus alone on the hills at night, communing with his Father. Jesus could persevere because of his dependence on his heavenly Father's love. He knew his Father so well that he was able to trust him totally, even in the face of such brutal evil, even when his whole being reeled with grief to the point of death.

The disciples here provide a picture of the opposite. Rather than persevering alongside Jesus, praying for and with him, and in turn being strengthened for their own roles in the unfolding drama, they fall asleep. They let human weakness – exhaustion, bewilderment, grief – dictate their action, or inaction. Prayerlessness led to failure in the time of testing.

Be warned.

Lord, strengthen me to be a faithful friend to those who solicit my prayers. Draw me into total dependence on you, that I might persevere as Jesus did, in the darkness of my deepest fears. Amen

MICHELE D. MORRISON

The catalytic converter

I thank my God every time I remember you. In all my prayers for all of you, I always pray with joy. (NIV)

I have to confess, for many people and situations on my prayer list, it would be truer for me to finish the sentence, 'every time I remember you', with 'my heart aches/sinks/is heavy'. When I think of prayer needs, my attitude is more one of begging than one of thanksgiving. Maybe that's why I can lose heart and go off the boil with prayer. The problem, rather than God, dominates my vision. Could gratitude be the key to persevering in prayer?

The focus of Paul's prayer for the Philippians is God. The Philippians are not problem-free. They are not perfect, mature believers, but Paul sees them through the lens of divine grace and loves them unconditionally, knowing that he who began a good work in them will carry it on to completion until the day of Christ Jesus (v. 6). Paul is in prison, yet he is full of gratitude and joy because he can see that as unlikely as it may appear in the flesh, a good outcome is guaranteed by the blood of Jesus.

It isn't that Paul ignores the problems the Philippians are experiencing. His words indicate that he is specific in his requests – which he makes with joy, because in every situation, he perceives opportunity for glorifying God. Problems enable revelation.

Hope – the confident expectation that God will turn up – should inspire our every prayer with anticipatory joy as we trust that God's answer always brings blessing. Gratitude is the catalytic converter that turns our prayer requests into songs of victory, even before the outcome is revealed.

Are you challenged by this thought? Comforted? Encouraged to double down on prayer by asking God to release in you a spirit of thanksgiving? I am.

Lord, I bring to mind a situation in my life, either past or present, which raises anxiety in me and leaches out the joy. Today, I give thanks to you for it, bring it before you in prayer and anticipate your perfect timing in the outcome. Amen
MICHELE D. MORRISON

Ask the tough questions... wait for the answers

But he [Thomas] said to them, 'Unless I see the nail marks in his hands and put my finger where the nails were, and put my hand into his side, I will not believe.' (NIV)

Don't you love Thomas? He isn't afraid to buck the trend. He isn't afraid to say what others – who, like him, weren't there in the upper room to see Jesus – might think. He doesn't couch his doubts in religious language; he says what he thinks. How could someone come back from death by crucifixion? 'Unless I see …'

God is not afraid of our questions. His words and his actions invite them. 'Ask and it will be given to you, seek and you will find; knock and the door will be opened to you' (Matthew 7:7–8). The great thing about Thomas is that, despite his passionate doubt, he waits for God. He perseveres. He is still there in the upper room a week later when Jesus reappears.

That must have been a long week! Jerusalem was a dangerous place for Jesus-followers to linger. Even those who had seen Jesus might have been getting restless. Some might have been considering the possibility that they had, in their grief, imagined their risen Lord. Maybe a kind of hallucination, a hysteria, had overcome them. Maybe Thomas was right…

Nevertheless, Jesus' followers hoped against hope. They persevered in their faith despite the apparent madness of the possibility of resurrection. They hung on to hope, stayed together and prayed like their lives depended on it.

Whatever it is you're struggling to believe just now, it probably isn't as outlandish as the truth that Jesus Christ was crucified, dead and buried… yet on the third day he rose again from the dead. Or maybe that's exactly what you're struggling with. Seek the Lord with all your heart and put all your hope in him. Persevere, like Thomas did. Spend time where you will encounter him. In the Bible. On your knees in prayer. In church. And wait.

Lord God, you know my fears, my doubts and my questions. Inspire me with zeal for truth; strengthen me to hold on to you and wait for the answers only you can give. Amen

MICHELE D. MORRISON

Don't give up!

Blessed are those who hunger and thirst for righteousness, for they will be filled. (NIV)

Many come into the kingdom of God via the road to Emmaus, but others come in on the road to Damascus. My childhood journey on the road to Emmaus led to a Damascus-road experience when I was grown and at a low ebb. Having sought a divine encounter for years, my homesick loneliness led me to a room crowded with people who knew Jesus and were singing their hearts out to him. I hungered and thirsted, and God filled me.

My initial response was to open the dusty Bible I had been given as a Sunday school child and read it, for the first time in my life. Every night, after putting our two pre-schoolers to bed, I would devour my Bible, encountering God in a personal way I had never dreamed possible. My husband wondered how long this would last. Would I persevere? I'm grateful to say that more than 40 years later I'm still leaning into scripture.

Key to faith is God giving people a hunger and thirst for him. Also key, though, are the believers who pray, who arouse hunger by sharing their testimonies, who create thirst by living a Jesus-based life which contrasts noticeably and attractively from a worldly-based life.

Jesus' sermon on the mount describes a way of life which is blessed by God but runs counter to common perceptions of a great life. Humility and poverty are never sought except by some cloistered orders. But rather than these characteristics bringing a life of misery, Jesus declares that they bring a life of pure joy.

It takes stamina and courage to live a counter-cultural life. There will be trolls; there will be mocking; there will be accusations and anger. We are called to be steadfast – loyal in the face of difficulties and doubts.

Lord, I pray that you will increase my hunger and thirst for you, so that I may be filled with your Holy Spirit who will speak life to those I meet. Amen
MICHELE D. MORRISON

Stop

Then Jesus said to them, 'The Sabbath was made to meet the needs of people, and not people to meet the requirements of the Sabbath. So the Son of Man is Lord, even over the Sabbath!' (NLT)

Beautiful symphonies vary their tempo between movements. Adagio and andante segue into allegro and vivace. Likewise, the music of life, as scored by our loving creator God is imbued with a cosmic rhythm.

As believers, we can become so conscientious in pursuit of justice, mercy or peace that we risk persevering to the point of breakdown. Two books I highly recommend on this subject are Bethany Hiser's *From Burned Out to Beloved* (InterVarsity Press, 2020) and John Mark Comer's *The Ruthless Elimination of Hurry* (Crown Publishing Group, 2019).

God took a break. After six wonderfully creative days, he rested. Moreover, in the Bible God sets out some rules to maintain health; remember the sabbath, he says. Jesus remembered the sabbath, despite the opposition's charges against him. He pulled aside to be alone with his nearest and dearest, to rest, play and worship. Many of us are driven by electronic alerts. Why not leave all devices in a cupboard once a week in order to focus on our Lord in complete delight and worship? God promises that when we turn to him, he will bless us with 'times of refreshment' (Acts 3:20). Doesn't that beat a spa day?

Comer suggests four elements of a sabbath break: stop, rest, delight and worship. Why do we find this so hard? One reason is because we have a supernatural enemy who actively works to foil our efforts, knowing that when we are well-rested, content and filled with love for God, we are impervious to his nefarious schemes.

Sabbath is not about sitting humourlessly in a pew for a few hours once a week. It is about reconnecting with the lover of our souls, renewing our spirits and refreshing our minds. Then we are equipped to persevere joyfully in the life God calls us to live.

Can you find a way to observe a weekly sabbath or take periodic sabbaticals, retreating for a couple of days to immerse yourself in the divine love of God?
MICHELE D. MORRISON

Don't let your hope flag

Rejoice in our confident hope. Be patient in trouble, and keep on praying. When God's people are in need, be ready to help them. Always be eager to practice hospitality. (NLT)

Perseverance has a negative connotation of dogged determination, suggesting a commitment to slave away in service, but that sort of perseverance will never stay the course. The perseverance that lasts comes from God: when we have given ourselves to him, he transforms our minds so that we can serve him eagerly and with joy. His gifts enable us to serve with supernatural strength and results.

Joy, patience and prayer. These are keys to living a successful Christian life. There is a situation I know of where a sincere Christian man is facing serious allegations, which could result in depriving him of his family, and even possibly lead to imprisonment. Throughout this lengthy ordeal, his eyes have remained on the Lord, the author and perfecter of his faith. He is facing this terrible time with inspirational courage, persevering in hope as he looks to God for vindication. He continues to worship in spirit and in truth. He, and his courageous wife, are beacons of faithfulness and love in the darkness.

There is much to draw on from this rich chapter in Paul's letter to the Romans. Notice the emphasis he puts on love and unity in the body of Christ. It is so important for us to encourage one another in the gifts we have been given. It is so important to honour one another, to be eager to help and offer hospitality with joy.

The final admonition of the chapter – 'don't let evil conquer you, but conquer evil by doing good' (v. 21) – is crucial to persevering in the Christian way. If we are to prevail, we must be alert to demonic challenges and quick to equip ourselves with the armour God gives us so that we can stand when the day of trouble comes.

Lord God, deliver us from evil, and strengthen us to persevere on the path of righteousness. Help us to encourage and aid our sisters to continue to walk the way of truth. Amen

MICHELE D. MORRISON

Don't look back

Forgetting what is behind and straining towards what is ahead, I press on towards the goal to win the prize for which God has called me heavenwards in Christ Jesus. (NIV)

What holds us back from a life of persevering faith? Sometimes it can be a guilty conscience about our past sins. But look at what Paul says, 'forgetting what is behind'. Few of us will have as serious a background as he had. He had held the coats of those who stoned Stephen to death. He had petitioned the Sanhedrin for letters to allow him to arrest Jesus-followers in Damascus, and headed off, breathing fire, in pursuit of those he saw as blasphemers. It must have taken a huge act of will and faith in the grace and mercy of our Father to be able to forgive himself and forget that.

Then he says, 'straining towards what is ahead'. Not just focused on, thinking about, or contemplating, but actively pushing forward, energetically straining for the goal: knowing Jesus. Knowing Jesus – this is what it's all about.

Paul's eager pursuit of Jesus, his overwhelming urge to know Christ and the power of his resurrection, is what inspired and provoked Paul to work ceaselessly in the service of the Lord. Then there is the curious and challenging statement that he wants to share in Christ's sufferings. This may mean many things, but one thing it no doubt means is that we must see our sinful nature crucified with Christ, hanging there in pain until it dies. As we allow God to destroy our sinful natures, we are emancipated, shedding the skin of our old ways and set free to live full and satisfying lives in his service.

Falling in love can be easy; staying in love requires relinquishing habits, accepting another point of view, humbling oneself. It involves our wills. Are you willing to surrender in order to pursue God relentlessly, straining to win the prize of knowing Jesus?

Lord, once again I lay down my life for you. Once again, I give you my plans, my hopes, my dreams and open my arms to receive from you all that you have for me. Amen

MICHELE D. MORRISON

Resigned or reconciled?

And being found in appearance as a man, he humbled himself by becoming obedient to death – even death on a cross! Therefore God exalted him. (NIV)

Continuing with yesterday's thoughts, today we're considering how Jesus' perseverance stemmed from his love for the Father, which led to his willingness to be humbled and obedient, even to death on a cross. It seems paradoxical that perseverance is fuelled by relinquishment. Why is this so important? Why does God look for us to surrender to him?

Nothing speaks with louder eloquence of utter faith in God's love than a willingness to entrust him with all that we are. Persevering in the Christian life is made possible as we allow the Holy Spirit to indwell us and take control.

A line I read in a novel recently has led me to ponder the nuance between resign and reconcile. The dictionary doesn't draw a very strong distinction between the two, stating that they indicate an acceptance of a situation a person cannot change. Was Jesus, finding himself in appearance as a man, resigned to his fate, or reconciled to it? Do such semantics matter? I suspect that they do. When I look at Jesus, I believe that, embracing the cross as the path chosen for him by his loving Father, Jesus demonstrated a loving reconciliation to the plan, trusting that God, being love, would only ever choose a way which led to a great outcome. Had he just resigned himself to the cross, I think his steps to Calvary might have metaphorically dragged reluctantly forward. His attitude exalted him to the right hand of the Father.

Perseverance flows in direct correlation to the measure of our love for God. It is of paramount importance that we nurture our relationship with him – studying scripture, meeting with other believers, praying, praising and worshiping. We can really persevere when we really love.

God, inspire my times with you. Lord, I know that I often approach your throne of grace in an offhand, disrespectful manner. Forgive me. I fall on my knees before you now. Amen

MICHELE D. MORRISON

Go, Christian, go!

Surrounded by such a great cloud of witnesses, let us throw off everything that hinders and the sin that so easily entangles. And let us run with perseverance the race marked out for us. (NIV)

I love the exuberance of this passage. It reminds me of the Kennedy Fitness Tests American kids did in school in the 1960s. One of the markers of fitness was a long-distance run. I hated long distance and would always approach the finish line completely exhausted. But when the girls on the sidelines started shouting, 'Sprint, Michele, sprint!', my pace quickened.

Encouragement is a necessity when it comes to persevering in the Christian life. We've looked at several of Paul's writings on perseverance, but we haven't mentioned that he often had Barnabas, the great encourager, at his side. The Christian life is not to be lived on our own. Part of God's concept of the ideal life is the family: not limited to the biological family but including the church family and friendship groups. One aspect of family I think it's important to mention is the intergenerational nature of it. We want those cheering us on to be our contemporaries as well as those older and younger; those filled with enthusiasm and optimism as well as those tempered and filled with a quiet wisdom and grace.

When my beloved sister died, age 37, a dear brother in Christ sought to comfort me by saying that now Judy was seated with Christ in the heavenlies, from where she could cheer me on. I was broken by her death, struggling to raise a young and growing family, and at the time at least, I didn't think heaven was a stadium with a bird's-eye view of our lives on earth: that would be hell as you watched loved ones struggling. You know, I'm not so sure anymore. Maybe Judy has been cheering me on these last 35 years.

Who do you see in the cloud of witnesses cheering you on: those who have gone before, maybe a spiritual mentor, the one who led you to Jesus, your family or those in your small group or church? Who are you cheering on?

MICHELE D. MORRISON

Rejoice in the Lord always

Consider it pure joy, my brothers and sisters, whenever you face trials of many kinds, because you know that the testing of your faith produces perseverance. (NIV)

Trials of many kinds come our way in life, trials which make Paul's admonition to consider them pure joy seem grotesque. Juvenile cancers and illnesses, stillbirths, wars, slavery, refugee situations: the world is full of horrors. How can we consider these opportunities for joy?

Perspective is key. Trials provide a chance to rip through the fabric of worldly understanding. As we draw close to God, he instils peace, restoring us and enabling us to glimpse his perspective. Remembering Jesus' sacrifice on the cross, knowing he hung there to do away with injustice and pain forever, our trust in him and appreciation for all he suffered and all he has accomplished deepens. However bad the trial is – and I have no wish to diminish the agony and anguish some trials bring – Jesus took it to the cross. Seeing it from the far side of the cross shrinks it and releases us to rejoice in the victory Jesus won. This is pure joy: seeing the profound triumph Jesus accomplished on the cross.

My current trials are pretty puny when measured against the major convulsions in the world, but they can become monsters as I feed them with my self-centred thinking. Yesterday I let things overwhelm me. As I prayed, asking God to help me gain his perspective, I was prompted to take a walk in the woods and fields around our home. I returned a new woman, as God, through his creation, restored me and readjusted my perspective.

As I have struggled to write this particular note, I've been listening to Jesus Culture's, 'Still in Control', and Kari Jobe's, 'I Am Not Alone'. Music can lift our spirits to align with his Spirit and restore joy. Walking and music help me to persevere.

Lord, when I walk through the valley of the shadow of death, you do not leave me or forsake me. Indeed, when I can walk no more, you carry me. Thank you, Jesus. Thank you. Amen

MICHELE D. MORRISON

Extreme headgear

Blessed is the one who perseveres under trial, because having stood the test, that person will receive the crown of life that the Lord has promised to those who love him. (NIV)

Is it right to motivate or be motivated by the promise of a reward? This verse suggests it is. So just what is the crown of life? Is it 'pie in the sky when you die'? Or is there something in this promise that pertains to the life you are living right now, here in the 21st century?

Jesus promised his followers that he came to give them life in all its fullness, rich and satisfying. Walking this earth inspired by truth, guided by God, filled with his Spirit, rejoicing in the incredible love that took Jesus through the most intense suffering any of us could ever imagine, let alone endure; is this not the crown of life?

Medieval artists often painted saintly people with a halo around their heads. Was this just imaginative license, or is there some truth in there being a visual manifestation marking followers of Jesus who have persevered under trial, quietly glowing with a confident trust in God?

Jesus said that those who were forgiven little, loved little. We all have much for Jesus to forgive, and maybe it all becomes clear when we are humbled, wrestling with attacks that strip us right down to the bare knuckles of faith.

Persevering through a time of severe trial anchors faith in the promises of God like nothing else can. As we submit, as we surrender to Jesus, he can more fully animate our lives and be revealed through them. He is our crowning glory; when we persevere under trial, the fruit of the Spirit, including joy, respond as if in a heated greenhouse, blooming with a vivacity and beauty we cannot fake.

The world notices.

We live our lives in seasons, some more targeted with pain than others. When we have persevered and are safely off the field of battle, we have the opportunity to encourage our sisters under fire.

MICHELE D. MORRISON

Lean on me, when you're not strong

We also glory in our sufferings, because we know that suffering produces perseverance; perseverance, character; and character, hope. And hope does not put us to shame. (NIV)

Here we are again. Paul is linking suffering and perseverance with joy. I wrote the other day that joy is a gift of the Holy Spirit, but it is also an act of will – a decision which, once made, takes root in our spirits and, as it grows, strengthens us. The joy of the Lord is your strength.

Suffering humbles us. It reveals our own inadequacy, which we independent-minded people don't like. One of the first statements I made as a toddler, according to my mother, was 'I can do it!' We are born with pride in our own abilities, and perhaps even the way we are brought up and bring up our children encourages that pride. When trials come though – illness and pain, broken relationships, false accusations – our inadequacy is laid bare. In extremis, we turn to God. We draw close to him and, as he promises, he cares for us. He designed us to be partners with him in life, and as we rely on him, we gain wisdom; our characters develop and our hope in him flourishes.

As we saw in Hebrews 12, we can be inspired and strengthened by others cheering us on. It is critical that we recognise that as the body of Christ, we are meant to support each other, especially during trials. My grandmother was widowed while she was carrying her sixth child. A few years later, she was conned out of the farm which she and my grandfather had scrimped and saved to buy. Heartbroken, living in a town where people kept their troubles to themselves, she took her own life. If she'd reached out to her church, would the outcome have been different? Maybe she did: I don't know. I just know she despaired and died alone.

Rejoicing in our sufferings is a tall order. We need each other if we are to develop the perseverance which leads to joy. Who needs your encouragement today?

MICHELE D. MORRISON

Service with a smile

Let us not become weary in doing good, for at the proper time we will reap a harvest if we do not give up. (NIV)

The Christian life is a journey, a pilgrimage. Thankfully, we are not always in the deserts and valleys. But as we saw yesterday, we are called to be alert to the needs and sufferings of others and be prepared to respond with a willing and generous heart and spirit.

This seems to be another statement with a reward to motivate us. Not a crown, this time, but the joy of reaping a harvest. Reaping a harvest at the proper time.

It can be discouraging to share your faith with others, hoping to excite faith in them, and then feel like nothing has happened. It's important to remember that you might be the one who has planted the seed, or watered it, but our Father is the gardener who grows faith in others. So this is an encouragement to those working in the mission field or even those sharing their lives with non-believers, not to grow weary and give up. God is never late. His timing is always perfect, though it may not seem like it to us.

On long marches, people sing songs. Life is a long march. Praise and worship help to encourage us and lift our tired spirits into a fresh engagement. They renew our faith in the God who threw stars into space, in the one who gave his only Son so that we might live forever with him. Raising a hallelujah bolsters our faith and encourages our hope and trust, and as such it becomes a weapon in our armoury against the temptations of the devil. Music is a definite encouragement whenever we grow weary.

Jesus asked his Father to send workers into the fields, which were ripe unto harvest. Look around yourself. Where do you see a field ripe unto harvest?

Lord, with the high praises of God in my mouth, I will lift your name on high and never give up. You are my God, and I will always love you. Amen

MICHELE D. MORRISON

Don't silence me!

'We must obey God rather than human beings!'… Day after day, in the temple courts and from house to house, they never stopped teaching and proclaiming the good news that Jesus is the Messiah. (NIV)

I am challenged by the apostles' courage. Here's Peter, who quaked in fear and lied when questioned by the slave girl on the night Jesus was arrested. He's horrifyingly familiar with the hideous torture of crucifixion, aware he could suffer the same fate. Yet now, miraculously released from prison by an angel of the Lord, Spirit-filled Peter and the other apostles set aside their human fears and head back to the temple courts to teach about Jesus.

Then, apprehended again by the temple guard, he and the others speak boldly to the Sanhedrin: we must obey God! Gamaliel advises that if the apostles are following a human agenda, they will fail, but if they are really obeying God, the Sanhedrin itself is in danger of coming up against the Almighty. It's enough to give the leaders pause for thought, so after flogging them, they admonish them not to speak any more about Jesus. How did they think that would be effective?

Throughout history, there have been times when church leaders have judged certain beliefs or practices heretical and banned, imprisoned or executed people. In our day, the Christian church is riven by division as people embrace one practice which others deem heretical. Surely it would be wise to follow the advice of Gamaliel, expecting that if the initiative is from God it will stand.

Despite Paul's instruction to obey the authorities of the jurisdiction in which we live, there are times when civil laws must be flouted. Making the distinction requires perseverance in hearing God's voice and having the courage to obey. There were many believers who defied the laws of Nazi Germany, even as organised religion sometimes colluded. Thousands of Jewish lives were saved by those who were willing to obey God rather than human rulers.

Mordecai asked Esther, 'Who knows but that you were born for such a time as this?' You and I were born for such a time as this. May we all persevere in our love for and service to Jesus.

MICHELE D. MORRISON

Thank you!

Fiona Barnard writes:

Thankfulness, like aspirin, is a surprisingly simple wonder drug. Many testify to it as a life-transforming antidote to unhappiness and disappointment. Ironically, a quick search of the internet will supply countless advertisements offering a way to secure the physical, emotional and psychological benefits of gratitude. In our day, it has become an industry in itself.

Yet how we need to learn gratitude! Our society tells us we deserve things. We are entitled. We should expect a certain standard of living, holidays in the sun and compensation if we don't get what we ordered. Our economy is built on jealousy, status and desire. We expend energy thinking about how we are going to spend the money we crave. We fill our homes with stuff. We do things we don't want to do in order to impress the people we don't like, all for personal advantage. Yet the feeling of emptiness grows. We ask, 'Why, when we are so comparatively rich, are we so often dissatisfied and depressed?'

Recently, I asked a Chinese student, with no background in faith, 'Why did you begin to think about God?' She smiled, 'I was so grateful that I wanted someone to thank!' It has been a tonic to walk alongside her as she has got to know the one who has given her so many gifts. The more she reads the Bible and discovers who Jesus is and what he has done, the more she wants to thank him with her words, her actions and now her life: in her last email, she called herself a Christian. She has God to thank.

In these next two weeks, we are reflecting on biblical gratitude: an attitude rooted in our response to the God who has given us everything we have and everything we need. It is a life lived in answer to this extravagant creator and Saviour and friend. It is a call from self-absorption to God-centredness, from manipulation to delight in his mercy. It is a habit we develop with the help of the Holy Spirit. It results in grace-filled thinking, speaking and living. As a bonus, we and those around us feel the better for it!

This year marks BRF's centenary and I am thankful for 21 years of writing for *Day By Day with God*: always daunting, always a privilege!

Thank you for your goodness and faithfulness!

Worship the Lord with gladness; come before him with joyful songs… We are his people… Enter his gates with thanksgiving and his courts with praise; give thanks to him and praise his name. For the Lord is good and his love endures for ever; his faithfulness continues through all generations. (NIV)

You can easily miss that unpromising grey door tucked between two brightly decorated shop windows. If you push it, you find yourself in a long shabby corridor with another door at the end. But that opens out into a little courtyard, and into the most delightful of gardens where there always seems to be flowers, even in the harshest of winters. It encircles the cottage of my friend who offers warmth and welcome.

Psalm 100 is one 'for giving thanks'. It invites us to 'come before him' (v. 2). There is a sense in which we have to make a journey past noisy attractions and distractions and through some gates. Our feet, whether skipping or sluggish, are taking us to worship the Lord. In the movement, we are preparing our hearts and focusing our thoughts. Through tattered corridors of daily muck and mess, through courtyards of ambiguity and uncertainty, hope and expectation, we enter into a place of safety, beauty, communion and joy. We arrive at a more conscious sense of the presence of our God who delights to welcome us there.

So what can we do but give thanks? Because he made us and because he loves us. Because he is good and faithful in all seasons, generations and forever. Because Jesus gave everything to save us, and the Spirit is closer than we can ever imagine. We may be alone as we come to thank him, but we join millions of others. Community thanksgiving encourages us when we struggle to worship and reminds us that 'the Lord is God' (v. 3). In song, our praise gladdens God's heart, and lifts our own. Gratitude multiplies our appreciation of the blessings which are ours in Christ.

'Enter his gates with thanksgiving': make that journey today, physically or in your imagination. Notice. Rejoice.

FIONA BARNARD

Thank you for your forever love!

Give thanks to the Lord, for he is good. His love endures forever. Give thanks to the God of gods. His love endures forever. Give thanks to the Lord of lords: His love endures forever. To him who alone does great wonders, His love endures forever. (NIV)

'Give thanks in all circumstances' is a refrain throughout the Bible. 'But how?' you may ask yourself. 'Other more spiritual people may manage it, but how about me?' That's when community worship can really help. Here we gather publicly with others to offer our thanks. We pray the songs and psalms that have sustained the Lord's people for millennia.

Although I do not come from a formal liturgical tradition, I am discovering the gift of set prayers. This psalm is a response of gratitude before all events of life. We are given a refrain that surrounds us as we worship our God together. It weaves its way through the panoramic account of creation and salvation: 'His love endures forever.' It puts God's decisive acts in the context of his commitment to us. It wraps itself around the truths we proclaim: 'His love endures forever.' It gets into our bones. It beats like a drum through the song. It interrupts – 'His love endures forever' – the sentences. It threatens to annoy us by not letting us get on with the narrative. It makes us stop and say: 'Why does this psalm keep repeating these words?' The answer comes back: 'His love endures forever.' In case we forget, in case we are distracted: 'His love endures forever.' Our response? Well, this liturgy of praise begins and ends with the cry 'Give thanks'.

How can we give thanks in all circumstances? Because 'his love endures forever'. Moon and stars, gifts of justice, mercy and abundance, all shout of his ongoing care for us. And when it's hard for us to give thanks and we cannot feel it, the community of worship carries us. His love endures forever.

How about writing your own liturgy of thanks, following the structure of Psalm 136?

FIONA BARNARD

Thank you for this feast every year!

'The Lord heard our voice and saw our misery, toil and oppression. So the Lord… brought us to this place and gave us this land, a land flowing with milk and honey; and now I bring the firstfruits of the soil that you, Lord, have given me.' (NIV)

Thank God for annual festivals when the calendar reminds us to stop and celebrate! It is so easy to get caught up in the everyday that we take for granted the potatoes and broccoli on our plates. In modern urban life, we may even forget that chicken and tomatoes do not originate in tins and packets! So happily, this is the season when people celebrate harvest thanksgiving in different ways across the world: with food and family and fun, with ritual and stories and generosity.

Even before the Israelites have set foot in the promised land, God gets their gastric juices gurgling. As they trudge through the desert, with daily heaven-sent quails and manna (a nutritious diet but not very varied!), he paints them a picture of plenty. He speaks of a time when they will have land to grow their own vegetables and grain. All gift. All grace. All God-given. Annual feasts will enable them to savour God's goodness to the core, chewing over their history, tasting the bitterness of slavery and suffering, before relishing the wonder of fresh home-grown fruit. That collective testimony will be recited by individuals bringing their harvest baskets to the temple. Each will declare allegiance to one who keeps his promise, who hears the cry of the oppressed and rescues them. Significantly, this Jewish feast is inclusive. They are to replicate God's generosity in sharing their bounty with foreigners and those without land.

Harvest, along with festivals like Advent, Christmas, Lent, Easter, Ascension and Pentecost provide annual opportunities to magnify gratitude. They mark times when we watch and wait and contemplate significant moments when God has touched history, and our own lives. We share these faith experiences through meals and memories, stories and songs, props and prayers. Our hearts burst with wonder.

What tokens of God's bounty would you put in your 'harvest thanksgiving' basket? Give thanks for those things now.

FIONA BARNARD

Thank you for being so generous!

'Yours, Lord, is the greatness and the power and the glory… we give you thanks… But who am I, and who are my people, that we should be able to give as generously as this? Everything comes from you, and we have given you only what comes from your hand.' (NIV)

'It's for you.' She presents you with a soggy scrap of paper and awaits your verdict. Anyone else might think, 'What on earth is this mangled mess of scribbles, squares and splodges? Now I am left with a paint box of brown sludge where once I had ten vibrant colours – and some of it has landed on my nice beige carpet.' But you exclaim, 'My dear: this is fantastic! Thank you so much. I love it. Is this you and me next to this wonderful house? You are so clever. I will stick this on my fridge.' She grins and feels like Picasso.

When King David gathers material to build a temple for God, he holds nothing back: gold and silver, precious stones and marble. The people follow his lead with wholehearted joy, adding treasures and skills to the project. The list of offerings is overwhelming and impressive. Yet it is David's prayer which is the most eloquent expression of his awestruck heart: the God of all gods, ruler of all things from everlasting to everlasting, has stooped to be their covenant Lord, to lavish on them all they are returning to him and to meet them in this temple. The maker of heaven and earth wishes to make his home among them. It is beyond comprehension.

'Everything comes from you, and we have given you only what comes from your hand' (v. 14). When a project is complete or a contract signed, at a graduation or a promotion, our gratitude is multiplied when we recognise God's gracious enabling. And, should we harbour an element of self-criticism, we can be sure that he accepts the soggy mess we offer and the heart behind it. 'This is fantastic,' he whispers, 'I love it' and pins it to his celestial fridge.

Can you think of one way, like David, you might encourage a community thanksgiving response to God's generosity?

FIONA BARNARD

Thank you for hearing me!

'In my distress I called to the Lord, and he answered me... When my life was ebbing away, I remembered you, Lord, and my prayer rose to you... I, with shouts of grateful praise, will sacrifice to you... I will say, "Salvation comes from the Lord."' (NIV)

Although I cannot claim to have ever found myself in the belly of a big fish, I recognise the vivid emotion Jonah describes in his prayer. That panic-filled sense of drowning in trouble and stress is not unfamiliar. You too may identify with bleak feelings of being entangled and trapped in desperate relationships or circumstances. Even today, you may wonder if you will ever again see the light of day.

What draws me to Jonah's prayer is that it is uttered 'while Jonah was inside the fish' (v. 1.): he is still in limbo, still suffering. The situation has given prayer an eloquent urgency, but also clarity. Although his life is still in peril and he remains far from where he would like to be, he realises that God has hold of him. Despite his wilful disobedience, God has saved him from a watery grave. At a time when worship of Yahweh was so focused on the Jewish temple, he has discovered the Lord in the depths of an ocean far from home. And so Jonah vows to be true to those promises he yelped in terror: he will yet sing songs of thanksgiving to the God who has not given up on him or let him go.

'Just thank God anyway,' I remember, as a pious teenager, instructing my unhappy father. His angry retort rendered my easy solutions questionable. I had to learn that we are not so much called to thank God for our trials, but called to learn to trace his hand in them. And in times when being grateful feels almost impossible, we are invited to imagine a day when we will thank God for his care (even in the belly of a smelly fish).

Tonight, before you sleep, look over your day and ask: 'What am I grateful for today?'

FIONA BARNARD

Thank you for your help in my work!

'He gives wisdom to the wise and knowledge to the discerning…
I thank and praise you, God of my ancestors: you have given me
wisdom and power, you have made known to me what we asked of
you, you have made known to us the dream of the king.' (NIV)

I wonder how often your job, colleagues and workplace have been the
subject of fervent petition and thanksgiving in your church. My experience is that we can be quite faithful at praying for the Sunday school,
community outreach and missionaries, but don't want to bother God (or
others) with nine to five office, supermarket and library concerns. Perhaps
consequently, we miss out on recognising God at work in these, our 'mission fields'.

   Daniel is a great model. His professional success is inseparable from
his prayerful dependence on God. Exiled to a pagan land, he keeps faith
central to his identity and vocation. He knuckles down to learn the craft
of government administration and excels in it. When he hears that the
king's advisors are to be killed for failing not only to interpret a troubling
dream but also to guess its contents, he acts with tact and decisiveness. In
a palace filled with foreboding, he asks the king for time, and his friends to
pray. God honours his trusting heart. During the night, the one who 'sets up
kings and deposes them' does indeed reveal both the dream and its meaning. Bursting with wonder, Daniel takes time to pour out his thankfulness
before reporting to the king. Daniel's experience of challenge and adversity
at 'the office' enlarges his appreciation of the Lord who gives 'wisdom to
the wise'. His friends are encouraged. The advisors are saved from execution. The king is awed by Daniel's 'Lord of kings' and promotes Daniel. Not
bad for a day's work!

   What workplace struggles have you and others faced? Can you recall
times when God intervened in response to prayer? How might the wonder
and gratitude of it spur you on to take further risks in his name and for
his glory?

---

*Thank God for the skills he has given you. Ask for strength and wisdom to
live out your gratitude so that colleagues, clients and communities may
be blessed.*

                                                          FIONA BARNARD

Thank you for the gift of family love!

'Excuse me, sir. Would you believe that I'm the very woman who was standing before you at this very spot, praying to God? I prayed for this child, and God gave me what I asked for. And now I have dedicated him to God. He's dedicated to God for life.' (MSG)

Pandemic lockdowns and facemasks have reminded us of the value of simple pleasures: a kiss, facial expressions, meals with those we love. We have also missed freedom to travel, a sense of control, family celebrations and more. Sometimes it takes not having something to realise how very much we want it. Significantly, we may also appreciate how the important things in life cannot be commanded: they can only be received as a gift.

Hannah longed for a baby more than anything. In a society which placed motherhood as a supreme good, she was unable to get pregnant. She saw children everywhere; even her own home was regularly invaded by the newborns produced effortlessly by her husband's other wife. All the love her husband lavished on Hannah did little to quench the yearning, the ache in the grind of his wife's taunts. Hannah's prayers seemed useless – until one day, she made a desperate deal: 'Lord, if you give me a son, I will return him to you.' The Lord met her there through the assurance of Eli the priest: 'Go in peace. And may the God of Israel give you what you have asked of him.'

Baby Samuel brought joy and pride and so much more. Every gurgle reminded her that Almighty God had heard her pitiful cry. He had removed her social shame. He had made her a member of the mothers' and toddlers' group. He had given her focus and purpose. So she worshipped him with a song of thanksgiving, but also with the most important thing in her life: Samuel himself. Her offering cost her dear: it was pure love because that was what she had received. Could Hannah have imagined how her private tale would inspire millions, including Jesus' mother Mary, to return their dearest to God the giver?

In view of God's generous gifts to you, what might you bring to him today as an offering?

FIONA BARNARD

92

Thank you for Jesus!

There was also a prophet, Anna… a widow… She never left the temple but worshipped night and day, fasting and praying. Coming up to them at that very moment, she gave thanks to God and spoke about the child to all who were looking forward to the redemption of Jerusalem. (NIV)

In your daydreams, do you hover mostly in the past or in the future? Recently, I wrote to a friend about regrets that resurfaced from reading an old diary. 'Thankfully, I haven't kept a record of yesteryear,' she replied. 'I'm looking ahead.' I am grateful to her for recalibrating my thinking, but I am also very conscious of God's gracious hand on my past mistakes and messes. I am so very thankful for that. It gives me hope for the future.

When we meet the elderly Anna in the Jerusalem temple, she has been a widow for decades. Alongside grief and disappointment, she will have experienced the challenge of survival in a society of male providers. Yet she is not really defined by her history. Instead, fresh each day, we see her persistent devotion to prayer. An open heart to hear God's voice has led to service as a prophet, speaking out what the Lord tells her. This day, she sees the elderly Simeon with a baby in his arms. She knows deep in her bones that this is the one for whom she has been longing and waiting. This child is Israel's promised Saviour. This scrappy bundle is the deliverer for a suffering, sinful people. And she gives thanks to God. She gives thanks for Jesus. She pours out her gratitude for answered prayer. Her delight spills over as she tells everyone about him. The more she speaks, the more she relishes the sheer wonder of what God has done and what this baby will do.

I love the way Anna's story embraces a past with much sadness and a hope-filled future. In the centre is the person of Jesus.

In this present moment, come to Jesus. Take time to gaze on him. Thank God for the gift he is to you and your community.

FIONA BARNARD

Thank you for forgiving me!

'She rained tears on my feet and dried them with her hair… she hasn't quit kissing my feet… she has soothed my feet with perfume… She was forgiven many, many sins, and so she is very, very grateful. If the forgiveness is minimal, the gratitude is minimal.' (MSG)

I don't remember much from my forays into Shakespeare, but there is one quote I often ponder. It comes from the mouth of King Lear, whose rash and foolish behaviour towards his daughters and his kingdom drives him mad and ranting into a thunderstorm: 'I am a man more sinned against than sinning.' It is not only school exams which ask, 'To what extent is this true?' Troubled individuals and stories in the news leave me asking, 'When people are so abused, is it any wonder they don't know how to treat others well? Where does responsibility lie? What is the place of forgiveness?'

This sensual story overflows with outrageous gratitude. It breaks all the rules of social etiquette and respectability. A 'sinful' woman, presumably the town harlot, thanks Jesus in the only way she knows: with her full body prostrated at his feet, unchecked tears, provocatively loose hair and expensive perfume. She doesn't care about the critical looks and self-righteous murmurs. Her full focus is on Jesus. She has received God's forgiveness through him. His mercy has gone deep into the dark crevices of her sin and suffering. In owning up to her wrongdoing, she has discovered that God's grace covers a lifetime of trouble and trauma and more. Overwhelmed and brimming with thankfulness, she returns all her love to Jesus.

When we make excuses for our cruel words and selfishness, we forfeit the joy of Jesus' forgiveness. Like Simon, Jesus' host that day, by dismissing rudeness or inhospitable thoughts as negligible in the face of 'bigger' sins, we discover our judgementalism coming back to bite us. Gratitude for our forgiveness should only increase our delight in being wondrously loved and valued! Such gratitude and delight can then show life-changing hope to a broken world.

What is your experience of Jesus' forgiveness? Thank him! Love him for it!

FIONA BARNARD

Thank you for healing me!

One of them, when he saw he was healed, came back, praising God in a loud voice. He threw himself at Jesus' feet and thanked him – and he was a Samaritan. Jesus asked, 'Were not all ten cleansed? Where are the other nine?' (NIV)

'Thank you!' says Mustafa, my 16-year-old student, every time our class finishes. I am always moved, because despite tragedy, this young lad retains a grateful outlook. He's a child refugee living in a foster home, far from all that is familiar: food, culture, language, friends. His parents and siblings disappeared during troubles in Sudan. Yet he smiles each English lesson and thanks me for my teaching.

The ten leprosy victims in our story have endured intense isolation and misery. Clawed hands, nerve damage and ulcers are not their only problems. Kept physically isolated for fear of contagion, they have missed the birth of nephews, weddings of sisters, deaths of grandparents. They have been barred from interaction with all save other medical pariahs. Word arrives that nearby there is a man with powers to heal. Standing at a distance, they beg this Jesus for pity. In response, he tells them to get themselves checked out by the priests who act as public health officers. On route, they are cleansed. Nine of them keep going, fuelled by adrenaline and astonishment, to see their mothers and employers and children. But one stops. He turns back to thank Jesus, flinging his whole healed body at his feet in thanksgiving. The wonder of his restoration overwhelms him and bursts out in worship of God: voice, body, heart.

That heartfelt gratitude means so much to Jesus. He commends the faith which strict religious Jews would refute in a despised Samaritan. Adding kind words of blessing to physical cure, he gives the man so much more than the nine whose excitement made them abandon the giver for the gift. That man gets to look into the tender eyes of God. He hears his restoring words of love. Grace upon grace.

How about going on a 'random acts of kindness' rampage today? Send a card, buy some flowers, cook a meal for someone – whether you think they deserve it or not!

FIONA BARNARD

Thank you for life!

Jesus, once more deeply moved, came to the tomb… they took away the stone… Jesus looked up and said, 'Father, I thank you that you have heard me. I knew that you always hear me, but I said this for the benefit of the people standing here, that they may believe that you sent me.' (NIV)

I like the growing trend for a funeral now to be called a 'service of thanksgiving'. There is something beautiful about gathering up a person's life and saying, 'Thank you, creator God: we are so glad you gave her breath.' Amid the tears, there is something deeply comforting in holding the person in memory, song, story and celebration, 'Thank you, Lord God: we are so grateful that we knew her.'

Jesus stands before the grave, tears rolling down his cheeks. His words of thanksgiving are spoken from a broken heart. He has just come from meeting his grieving friends Martha and Mary whose brother Lazarus has died. The community watch, amazed at the deep love he has for the family and his pain at their loss. Death is cruel: it was never meant to be like this. However, we who know what happens next must never let that detract from the anguish and anger Jesus feels in this cemetery.

I find Jesus' prayer intriguing. He thanks the Father for listening to him, for hearing what could only have been profound distress. He knows that the Father is always attentive to him, whether to words or wordless cries. We glimpse the intimacy of their relationship. He has not been abandoned in his sorrow. We hear the Son's dependence on the Father. And now there is more: Jesus knows his petition that Lazarus be restored to life has been answered, perhaps because there is no stench of decomposition when the stone is rolled back. This time, the Father has said 'yes' so that those at the grave might believe in Jesus as the one sent from God. Yet Jesus knows that very soon, in the face of death, the Father will say 'no'. All for us: so that in Christ, we pass through death to unfettered life.

Recall the life of someone for whom you are grateful: what was it about them that made such an impact on you?

FIONA BARNARD

Thank you for your presence with us!

When he was at the table with them, he took bread, gave thanks, broke it and began to give it to them. Then their eyes were opened and they recognised him, and he disappeared from their sight. They asked each other, 'Were not our hearts burning within us while he talked with us?' (NIV)

I really am grateful for the food in front of me: I love the smell and colours, the texture and tastes of dinner. Living near both farmland and seaside, I am thankful for those who grow the corn and pick the strawberries and catch the fish. My local supermarkets stock produce from around the world, bringing gifts, challenges and hardships to my trolley. Yet often I catch myself mouthing a mealtime grace as a quick unthinking prelude to the real business of eating. A lifetime's habit can become alarmingly shallow.

What is it about this grace which has such a dramatic impact on Cleopas and his friend? They have walked a long way with Jesus. They have shared their bewildered emotions. They have heard him open up scriptural truths as never before. Their hearts are burning. Yet it is at their own ordinary table that everything changes. They finally recognise him: when he takes the bread, gives thanks for it, breaks it and hands it to them.

Those four verbs – took, gave thanks, broke and gave – are echoes of earlier stories. It is what Jesus did when he fed the multitudes (Luke 9:16) and on the night before his death (Luke 22:19). It is his habit to receive food as a gift, to acknowledge the giver before sharing it with those around him, whether thousands of strangers or the closest of friends. Somehow, in word and act, he is both host and guest. In prayer, he brings wonder and gratitude, recognition and revelation to meals. In this grace, we too are invited to notice the nail-scarred hands of the risen Christ, to hear the ever-grateful heartbeat of the Son: taken, broken, given for us. Communion at the supper table: layers of thanksgiving amid munching and chat.

Imagine an Emmaus table in your house. Perhaps you can lay an extra place for Jesus. Watch what he does. This meal, and every meal, is holy. Thank him.
FIONA BARNARD

Thank you for comforting me!

Rejoice in the Lord always… in every situation, by prayer and petition, with thanksgiving, present your requests to God… I have learned to be content whatever the circumstances… I can do all this through him who gives me strength… Yet it was good of you to share in my troubles. (NIV)

'The time I had in prison was the real freedom for me,' claims Taher, a Middle Eastern Christian, now living as a refugee in Turkey. Despite having lost house, work, homeland, family and material possessions, his wife Donya adds, 'Jesus is worth everything'. Reading their story in a recent magazine of *Open Doors*, which supports persecuted Christians, puts my petty concerns into perspective.

It reminds me of Paul's words in his letter to the Philippians. Written from jail, when there was little concept of humane conditions and rights for prisoners, it is nonetheless regarded as his most joyful epistle. It leaves me wondering, 'For what can he be grateful, stuck for months in a rotten jail?' Philippians offers some hints. Alongside acknowledging sorrow (2:27), hunger and need (4:12), Paul speaks of praying constantly. Instead of complaining, 'Lord, you owe me!', he has learnt contentment. He determines to be joyful *in the Lord*. He celebrates the spread of Jesus' gospel (not his!). He focuses on godly purity and truth (4:8). And so, in this battle of the mind, he finds Christ strengthening his heart and giving astonishing peace.

Perhaps we listen more attentively to those who ooze gratitude and grace amid suffering. Whether physical walls or circumstances imprison, prayer and contentment are secret ingredients in genuine thankfulness. Yet there is also a very tangible encouragement for Paul: not only does he see God at work in the Philippians, but he is profoundly grateful for their financial provision and their sending gentle Epaphroditus to support him. What an added privilege is ours when we, like the Philippians, can bring God's practical comfort to others!

How might you tackle an increasingly entitled mindset with a grateful heart? Today, can you reach out to someone 'in chains'?

FIONA BARNARD

Thank you for everything!

'Praise and glory and wisdom and thanks and honour and power and strength be to our God'… 'he who sits on the throne will shelter them with his presence. "Never again will they hunger; never again will they thirst"… "And God will wipe away every tear from their eyes."' (NIV)

I could never have foreseen it, but the moment my mother died, I understood hope in a new way. This greatly loved body lay before me, motionless after a long struggle. Yet somehow, a deeper reality surfaced as I found the night nurse: 'I think she has gone. But I am a Christian. I will see her again alive.' In that sterile hospital, I caught a glimpse of another tantalising reality, a dimension full of God's tender presence. Amid bemused grief, a surprising joy and gratitude emerged.

At a time of looming persecution with many incentives to compromise faith in Jesus, John pulls back the heavenly curtain. He ushers frightened and resigned believers into the very throne room of Almighty God. Like an impressionist artist, he paints the indescribable in awe-inspiring brushstrokes. 'Don't give up!' he cries. 'You are weeping now. You are tired and weather-beaten, hungry and thirsty, but this will all end. Stay with Jesus and you will overcome. Can you see these people in white robes waving palm branches in delight? These are tokens of their victory: Jesus really has saved them. He has brought each one through crushing trials. Look: the lamb has become their shepherd and all their suffering, like his, is over. Nothing has been wasted. The pain is not minimised: God sees each precious tear but is wiping them from their eyes. This is a bright new beginning, full of wonder, of worship, of thanksgiving.'

Some days, gratitude is spontaneous; other times, it is a gritted discipline, almost beyond what we can muster. This vision lifts our eyes to the slain lamb. We may not understand his ways now, but one day, Christ-centred hope will unfurl its multicolour wings of glory: faith will become sight. Our thanksgiving will resonate across the universe for evermore.

What do you take away from this series on gratitude and thanksgiving?

FIONA BARNARD

Advent hope

Helen Williams writes:

It's Advent Sunday and the call to wake from sleep and be ready to greet Jesus, the baby born in Bethlehem and the king returning in glory, will ring round our places of worship today. I love this season, though it's often an extraordinarily busy time with all sorts of pressures. We have four weeks though to wait, to watch, to prepare, to check our hearts and priorities, to inhabit the hope we have in Jesus.

To help us do this we're going to use an Advent tradition (which may well have been in use as early as the 5th century), the 'O' Antiphons. These short sentences were originally sung in monasteries and are now used in many churches and cathedrals too, one sung each day from 16 – 23 December. Each antiphon greets the Messiah with a title that describes him and is rooted in Isaiah's prophecies. They all end with a prayer of hope. The 'O' before each name for Jesus is what makes them the 'O' antiphons! I wonder if this exclamation of 'O', and with it a renewed wonder at our incredible Saviour, could stay on our lips throughout this season as we draw others into these promises of hope.

One of the rather delightful things about the antiphons is that in their original Latin (you'll find these in the titles for each note), you could take the first letter of each of the seven names for Jesus, assemble them in reverse order, and they would spell out the phrase, 'ERO CRAS' which means 'Tomorrow I will be there'! It's the cry of the Bridegroom in answer to our Advent cry, 'Maranatha' or 'Come, Lord Jesus'.

May he call to us afresh as we let these seven antiphons guide us through this first week of Advent. If you weren't aware of them before, you will probably recognise five of the themes eventually worked into the carol, 'O come, O come, Emmanuel'. You may like to look this up and I pray that as you sing this carol this Christmas it may come alive for you in a new way. May your journey through this Advent, whatever your circumstances, bring you into a new and deeper awareness of the God who was and is and is to come, and is the reason for our hope.

O Wisdom! (O Sapientia)

The wisdom that comes from heaven is first of all pure; then peace-loving, considerate, submissive, full of mercy and good fruit, impartial and sincere. Peacemakers who sow in peace reap a harvest of righteousness. (NIV)

> *O Wisdom, coming forth from the mouth of the Most High, reaching from one end to the other mightily, and sweetly ordering all things: Come and teach us the way of prudence.*

Whether it was Charlotte, the extraordinary spider in *Charlotte's Web* or C.S. Lewis' breathtaking lion, Aslan, there was always one character in every childhood book to whom others went for wise counsel and I so wanted to be like them. Many chapters of the Bible are devoted to examining and describing wisdom. 'Where then does wisdom come from?' asks Job (Job 28:12), answering his own question: 'The fear of the Lord – that is wisdom' (v. 28). The psalmist too asks that God would 'teach us to number our days, that we may gain a heart of wisdom' (Psalm 90:12).

When God asks Solomon what gift he needs, Solomon asks for wisdom (or a 'discerning heart') to be able to rule well. God gave him other gifts too, so pleased was he that Solomon had first sought wisdom (1 Kings 3:9). Isaiah prophesied that the Messiah would have the 'spirit of wisdom' (Isaiah 11:2) and be 'excellent in wisdom' (28:29). When we meet him in the pages of the New Testament we realise that Jesus himself is the embodiment of wisdom. From childhood he had grown in wisdom (Luke 2:52) and, as Paul writes, he 'has become for us wisdom' (1 Corinthians 1:30).

In our first antiphon we proclaim the source and eternal reach of wisdom, asking that wisdom teach us 'prudence' (good sense). What we often prize is knowledge, know-how and the power to control. As our verses describe, godly wisdom is the very opposite of this. It bears a remarkable likeness to the description of the fruit of the Spirit in Galatians 5.

This Advent 'Come, Lord Jesus', our wisdom, and 'sweetly order' our lives: our time, our work, our hospitality, our preparations and celebrations, our strivings, our loneliness and our weakness. Be our wisdom in all things. Amen
HELEN WILLIAMS

O Adonai!

But Moses said to God, 'Who am I that I should go to Pharaoh and bring the Israelites out of Egypt?' And God said, 'I will be with you.' (NIV)

> *O Adonai, and leader of the House of Israel, who appeared to Moses in the fire of the burning bush and gave him the law on Sinai: Come and redeem us with an outstretched arm.*

I love the story of Moses and the burning bush and often find myself turning back to it. I'm inspired by this direct encounter with the living God in an ordinary, everyday kind of place which becomes too holy even for shoes – it becomes a place of reminder, promise, calling, honesty and equipping.

Our second antiphon reminds us of the thread running through the whole of scripture: that of God's action in leading his people from slavery to freedom and his faithful care through good times and bad. God reminds Moses he's always been there for his people since the time of Abraham and that he will go on delivering them from oppression. 'Adonai' was the word used in place of God's name in Ancient Israel. It means 'My Lord'. This Lord is 'I am who I am'. He was and he will be – Adonai – our Lord, leader and redeemer. Past, present and future.

Encountering God's presence and hearing his call, Moses is a jittering heap of nerves! There is an endearing honesty here as Moses wheedles and God encourages. How many times have you and I been in this place, sensing God wants us to do something and yet feeling hopelessly inadequate? Yahweh later promises Moses that he will rescue Israel 'with an outstretched arm' (24:12). From our New Testament vantage point though, we know there is much more rescuing to be done and that ultimate freedom is won as Jesus stretches out his arms of love on the cross.

Spend a moment asking the Holy Spirit to illuminate where you might be enslaved – maybe wrong or unhelpful attitudes, habits, expectations or relationships. Hear the voice of Adonai offering you his forgiveness and freedom.

HELEN WILLIAMS

O Root of Jesse! (O Radix Jesse)

A shoot will come up from the stump of Jesse; from his roots a Branch will bear fruit. The Spirit of the Lord will rest on him – the Spirit of wisdom and of understanding, the Spirit of counsel and of might. (NIV)

> *O Root of Jesse, standing as a sign among the peoples; before you kings will shut their mouths, to you the nations will make their prayer: Come and deliver us, and delay no longer.*

The people of Israel saw David's reign as a sort of golden age of relative security between turbulent times. By the time Isaiah is writing, Jerusalem has been destroyed and God's people are in exile. Jesse's stem has indeed been cut down to a stump. It was hard to believe that it would ever flower again. Isaiah offers a message of hope – God will deliver his people and save them. Their Messiah will not come in glory but 'like a tender shoot and a root out of dry ground' (Isaiah 53:2), and yet he will be someone before whom kings will be rendered speechless (Isaiah 52:15).

When we see the horrific devastation caused by forest fires, it's miraculous that green shoots do ultimately push through grey ash. Often roots below ground remain strong and full of potential for life and growth. This is how it was with the stump of Jesse. This antiphon reminds us once again of God's faithfulness, his power and his initiative for rescue and salvation. Like the people of Israel, we might find it hard to maintain hope in the face of often unrelenting bad news and difficult to imagine how God is going to bring about his salvation, but cultivating that shoot of hope is an absolute imperative for us as Christians. Once again this Christmas we will celebrate the God who came among us with the sole purpose of loving us and saving us. This is the hope we must offer our world.

May you, 'being rooted and established in love', have the power 'to grasp how wide and long and high and deep is the love of Christ, and to know this love that surpasses knowledge' (Ephesians 3:17–19).

HELEN WILLIAMS

O Key of David! (O Clavis David)

These are the words of him who is holy and true, who holds the key of David. What he opens no one can shut, and what he shuts no one can open. (NIV)

> *O Key of David and sceptre of the House of Israel; you open and no one can shut; you shut and no one can open: Come and lead the prisoners from the prison house, those who dwell in darkness and the shadow of death.*

I wonder if you've seen the highly acclaimed film, *Paddington 2*. Without wanting to spoil it if you haven't, what the kind little bear does to reform a prison by making marmalade sandwiches is quite remarkable (and worth seeing!). What Jesus, the key of David, does though, is not merely make our prison a bit more comfortable. No, he offers us a way out of our imprisonment, opening 'wide our heavenly home' as the carol 'O Come, O come Emmanuel' says, and making 'safe the way that leads on high'. He is the key to our heavenly future (and present) and, as we confess our sin, he also locks the door on that, closing 'the path to misery'.

The Bible begins and ends with the closing of one door and opening of another: in Genesis 3, the door is closed on paradise, but in Revelation 4 and 19 we see a doorway open into heaven, with the sense of hope and thrill about the full reign of Jesus the king. In our passage from Revelation 3, the one who now holds the key of David is the risen Jesus – the words of Isaiah's prophecy (Isaiah 22:22) at last coming to fruition. Jesus, the key of David, has opened the door to the heavenly kingdom and the door remains open because of the Philadelphians' faithfulness to Jesus. I love that God shows he understands their weakness though, exhorting them to 'Hold on'! Sometimes it's all we can do – hold on to Jesus until we see his victory and begin to understand our freedom.

Do pray the last two lines of this antiphon both for yourself and for anyone whom God puts on your heart: 'Come and lead the prisoners from the prison house, those who dwell in darkness and the shadow of death.'

HELEN WILLIAMS

O Morning Star! (O Oriens)

Arise, shine, for your light has come, and the glory of the Lord rises upon you. See, darkness covers the earth and thick darkness is over the peoples, but the Lord rises upon you and his glory appears over you. (NIV)

> *O Morning Star, splendour of light eternal and sun of righteousness: Come and enlighten those who dwell in darkness and the shadow of death.*

We once took our children backpacking through Egypt. Courageously, we agreed to climb Mount Sinai while there. It was pitch-black and freezing cold as we began our climb at around 2.00 am, but after an arduous few hours we found ourselves, shivering in thin blankets, sitting on a rock at the summit. As the darkness drained from the inky black sky, we watched the Morning Star appear, shining in all its glory, and gradually a warm pink glow bathed the mountaintops stretching into the distance. As dawn gave way to morning, we were suffused with warmth and light.

The stark contrast of light and dark is here in this shortest antiphon, set for 21 December – the shortest day. In it we ask Jesus, our bright Morning Star (Revelation 22:16), our Sun of Righteousness (Malachi 4:2) and our Splendour of Light (Psalm 104:1–2) to dispel the world's darkness. Isaiah addressed a people invaded, subjugated by a foreign power and taken into exile. Life was precarious and vulnerable, and when Isaiah talks about 'thick darkness', he is speaking of this disorientation and helplessness.

As we look into our own world's darkness, we know that, for many, hope is an alien concept. If we are serious about our celebration of Jesus – God with us – this Christmas, it is not enough to just hope for the best for our world. Isaiah is clear, the victory does belong to the God of Light and as his people inhabit that light, so others will be drawn into it. We have to be hope-full for God's rule of light and life.

'O, come, thou Dayspring, come and cheer our spirits by thine Advent here. Disperse the gloomy clouds of night and death's dark shadows put to flight.' Amen

HELEN WILLIAMS

O King of the Nations! (O Rex Gentium)

'See, I lay a stone in Zion, a chosen and precious cornerstone, and the one who trusts in him will never be put to shame.' Now to you who believe, this stone is precious. (NIV)

O King of the nations and their desire, the cornerstone making both one:
Come and save the human race, which you fashioned from clay.

Our sixth Advent 'O' antiphon addresses God as 'King of the nations' – a direct quote from Jeremiah 10:7, where Jeremiah reminds God's people that 'among all the wise leaders and in all their kingdoms' there is no one like their God – the king of kings! He is also 'the desire of nations' (remember the carol 'Angels from the realms of glory' as sages are exhorted to abandon their contemplations in search of him). There's the sense here that, as Augustine so beautifully articulated, 'Our hearts are restless until they find their rest in you.'

Our king of kings is also described as the cornerstone – predicted by the psalmist (Psalm 118:22); prophesied by Isaiah (28:16); quoted by Peter (Acts 4:11) and echoed by Paul in Ephesians 2:20. In his first letter, Peter, writing to the churches in Asia Minor, picks up this theme, describing how, as we come to the living stone, we will together be built into the body of Christ with him as the critical cornerstone. It's all about unity. Both the Advent assertion that Jesus is king of the nations and the fact that he is the unifying cornerstone remind us of God's creation intention, the oneness of the human race, all made from the same dust, all given an equal part in our world. We're not supposed to be fragmented or fighting but to live in peace, led by the one true king. This passage in 1 Peter reminds us that Jesus is a king like no other – he is no power-hungry ruler, but the one who brought us into being, loves those he created and is 'the shepherd and overseer of [our] souls'.

'You have made us for yourself, O Lord, and our hearts are restless until they find their rest in you.' King Jesus, may we find that rest and unity this Advent as we let you be the cornerstone of our lives. Amen

HELEN WILLIAMS

O Emmanuel!

All this took place to fulfil what the Lord had said through the prophet: 'The virgin will conceive and give birth to a son, and they will call him Immanuel' (which means 'God with us'). (NIV)

O Emmanuel, our King and our lawgiver, the hope of the nations and their Saviour: Come and save us, O Lord our God.

In the opening chapter of the New Testament, Matthew explains: 'There were fourteen generations in all from Abraham to David, fourteen from David to the exile to Babylon, and fourteen from the exile to the Messiah.' Everything has been leading to this moment! From the beginning, God has been working out his plan to save his people. He had given Moses his rules for life in the ten commandments and, though his people repeatedly ignored him, God went on rescuing them and promising them salvation. Now the time is right for Emmanuel, the ultimate Saviour, to appear, the one foretold by Isaiah (Isaiah 7:14).

This week we have met Jesus – our wisdom; Lord; life-giving root; key to freedom; dark-dispelling Morning Star; King, and now Immanuel – God with us. We see throughout scripture how God created us to be with him: his walking in the garden; the tabernacle in the camp; the ark of the covenant among the army; the temple in the city centre; the bread of the presence; the fiery pillar; the Shekinah; the Son of Man walking among the lampstands; the Holy Spirit. He wants to be our God; he wants us to be his people. The Bible ends right where it begins: 'I heard a loud voice from the throne saying, "Look! God's dwelling place is now among the people, and he will dwell with them. They will be his people and God himself will be with them and be their God"' (Revelation 21:3). From beginning to end, from the first coming of Jesus to his second coming, the message of hope is clear – God is for us, and God is with us.

An Advent blessing: May 'Christ the Sun of Righteousness shine upon you, scatter the darkness from before your path, and make you ready to meet him when he comes in glory.' Amen

HELEN WILLIAMS

Zechariah: blessing, encouragement and hope

Anne Le Tissier writes:

The minor prophets may not be everyone's go-to books of the Bible, not least Zechariah with its vivid imagery and, at times, seemingly bizarre symbolism. His words may appear confusing to interpret or to apply to daily life, but Zechariah's overall theme of blessing, encouragement and hope is an uplifting message from God.

At the outset of his ministry, Zechariah prophesied alongside Haggai (roughly 520BC). Together, they encouraged the returned exiles from Babylon to repent of their lax attitude towards rebuilding the temple in Jerusalem, while assuring them of God's blessing as they recommitted themselves to his ways. But Zechariah's prophetic anointing also embraced a longer-term view of the coming of the Messiah and his kingdom. God's sovereignty over nations, powers and history itself, remained indisputable.

Although Zechariah didn't write in a linear fashion and repeated certain themes, you may find it useful to know that the book is basically in three parts. First, an introduction (1:1–6). Second, eight visions that Zechariah received in one night (1:7–6:8), offering meaning to the Israelites present but also providing a glimpse of things to come, plus a 'bonus' vision and explanation (6:9–8:23). Third, two collections of poetry and prophecy conveyed in a different style, concerning the messianic kingdom (9–14).

Zechariah is an ideal book to be reading in December as it is powerfully prophetic of Christ's first and second coming – grounding our Advent and Christmas preparations in God. But as we begin, may I invite you to mull on the following questions which may prepare your heart for God's whispers through the message of his faithful prophet. Where are you in your relationship with God: intimate, yearning for more, disinterested, aloof? Are you intentionally yielding to the ways God wants to transform you into his image, or feeling indifferent? Persevering or discouraged by life's problems and setbacks? Inspired by, dedicated to, or lacking enthusiasm for God's kingdom priorities and calling on your life?

No one will respond perfectly to these questions, not least me. They are simply a prompt to help us evaluate our walk with God; to open our hearts afresh to his love for us and to our life in Christ that he longs for us to experience in greater measure.

God is for you

'Return to me,' declares the Lord Almighty, 'and I will return to you'…
So the Lord spoke kind and comforting words to the angel who
talked with me… 'My towns will again overflow with prosperity, and
the Lord will again comfort Zion and choose Jerusalem.' (NIV)

Reading Zechariah can feel like a dizzy fairground ride, but the questions from the introduction may help you discern how God wants to encourage you.

God was speaking to the returned exiles enduring a tough life back in Jerusalem; their struggles to rebuild their homes, livelihoods and the temple were distracting them from his commands. Perhaps we can relate to this with our own struggles at home, work or in our relationship with God. If so, see how he urged them to return to him – not just to his law or his way of life, but to *him*; to a devoted relationship, part of which involves yielding to his holy ways.

God then encouraged them with the first two visions. The horseman symbolised his attentive watch over the world, comforting and assuring his people of his enduring, passionate protection and care, in all their circumstances. God reminded them of his sovereignty over all nations, no matter how vast, controlling and powerful they might appear. His anger rested on those who had oppressed Israel (the four horns), and he would raise up 'the craftsmen' to scatter them as they had first scattered his people.

God is still for you, not against you. He loves you immeasurably more than you may realise and will never abandon you. He longs that you may encounter him more fully in your life and desires to work in and through you; influencing others through your work, creativity, relationships and productivity – whatever shape or form these may take.

Doubts and a sense of failure or inadequacy may hound you, but God speaks truth to dismiss any lies, shaming or blaming that are holding you back. Draw close to him now in prayer.

Father God, thank you. Your unwavering, passionate love and forgiveness
draw me to you with relief and gratitude. Please search my heart and mind
and show me where I'm not trusting you, or not walking in your ways. Amen
ANNE LE TISSIER

Security in God's unseen presence

'I myself will be a wall of fire around it,' declares the Lord, 'and I will be its glory within… Many nations will be joined with the Lord in that day and will become my people. I will live among you.' (NIV)

We can't always see tangible evidence confirming why we should trust God's invisible yet protective and empowering presence. He may be calling us to lead a group, to teach or preach, to reach out to someone we don't know very well, to take on a challenging role or to share our faith with others at the risk of being ridiculed or opposed. But following on from yesterday's message, God promises to be with us always and to provide all we need – and this is the crux of chapter 2.

Jerusalem and God's temple would be rebuilt, though not for Israel alone. Zechariah prophesies about a city without boundary walls (2:2–5). The inhabitants would therefore feel vulnerable because of many enemies that oppressed it, but it's an image that symbolises God's higher plan to welcome all nations to his presence.

Could the Israelites really trust in God's unseen presence to protect them more than stone walls? Would his unseen glory be their source of power and productivity, of assurance and purpose, rather than their felt capabilities, resources and reputation? And would God's infinite love and desire that all peoples would come to know him, be sufficient motivation to inspire them out of their self-centred preoccupation for protection and provision? These intrinsic questions prompted by the text speak to our hearts today.

'Have courage!' and 'Fear not!' are commands repeated throughout scripture but perhaps we look to 'walls' for security. Our 'walls' might be such things as finances, abilities, experience, reputation or certain relationships. Ultimately, these are fallible, but this vision inspires us to turn our hearts to God's infallible promises, his constant presence and his heart for all people to be saved.

What 'walls' do you rely on for perceived security? What 'glory' do you seek affirmation and contentment from? Talk with God about these, then immerse your heart in the security and assurance of his presence with you now.

ANNE LE TISSIER

Speak life, not lies

'The Lord rebuke you, Satan! The Lord, who has chosen Jerusalem, rebuke you! Is not this man a burning stick snatched from the fire?' Now Joshua was dressed in filthy clothes… Then he said to Joshua, 'See, I have taken away your sin, and I will put fine garments on you.' (NIV)

When we respond proactively to the truth that God is for us (see Sunday) and the promised security and provision of his presence (see Monday), we can expect spiritual opposition (Ephesians 6:12). Zechariah speaks of Satan, meaning 'adversary'; a doctrine developed more fully in the New Testament, which describes him as a thief and the father of lies. So, when you find your responses, behaviour, outlook or faith are being shaped and led by self-talk that blames, shames, slanders, undermines or condemns, and when you start to believe outright lies about who you are, pay attention to the fact that these thoughts do not reflect God's truth.

In Zechariah's fourth vision, Joshua, the high priest at the time, stood before God on behalf of the people who were guilty of sin. But God took it upon himself to remove the sin and reclothe him in fine, i.e. heavenly, holy, garments; the prophetic anticipation of the person and work of Joshua's greater namesake, Jesus, through whom every believer can directly approach God's presence (Hebrews 4:14–16).

If we are persistently living in opposition to God's character and commands, then it's time to make a choice about whom we truly believe in and yield to as Lord. Some of us, however, may be sincere in seeking to live well for God, yet battle with false perceptions of inadequacy or rejection from his purposes. We may feel shame, condemnation or spiritual impoverishment. If so, let's be mindful to speak out, 'the Lord rebuke you, Satan!' Let's speak truth to our heart, mind and soul. And let's adopt Christ's own resistance to the taunts and temptations, 'Away from me, Satan!', declaring appropriate truth from God's word to defeat Satan's accusations.

Thank you, Jesus, for removing my sin and shame, for clothing me in your righteousness and uniting me with God. I confess […]. I receive your forgiveness. Help renew my heart and mind with your truth. Amen

ANNE LE TISSIER

Our power source

'This is the word of the Lord to Zerubbabel: "Not by might nor by power, but by my Spirit," says the Lord Almighty.' (NIV)

My days are filled with all kinds of roles, responsibilities and activities, but today's reading challenges me: for whom am I doing, pursuing and fulfilling these things? And the answer may be found in the extent to which I look to and lean on God to infuse them with his presence.

Zechariah reminds God's people that the empowering of his Spirit is fundamental to the completion of his temple, for it was far more than a building to offer sacrifice, prayer and praise. The temple was built as a witness to God dwelling with his people; the light from the golden lampstand reflecting the glory of his presence. No 'might' nor 'power' – no skill, wealth or sheer hard work – could achieve or manufacture this. Only God's Spirit could imbue the bricks and mortar building with its divine ethos and purpose, a truth symbolised by the abundant supply of oil from the olive trees. And it was God's Spirit who directed and anointed the ministry of the temple's priestly and ruling officials (represented by Joshua and Zerubbabel); roles that would one day combine in the fullness of God dwelling in Jesus.

Today we are living temples of God's Spirit. Our role is not to impress people with who we are or what we do, but to be yielded vessels for God to impress himself on others: his love, grace, beauty, goodness, wisdom and truth. And we cannot achieve that through our own efforts, skills or resources. We offer all that we are and do to serve God, but ultimately, it's our yielding to his enlightening and empowering presence in us that reveals who he is and draws others to him; even in the seemingly 'small things' of our lives (v. 10).

Consider your home, skills, roles and relationships. God wants to bring beauty, blessing and hope to every part of your life. Prayerfully recommit yourself to pursuing and yielding to the Holy Spirit in all you say and do.

ANNE LE TISSIER

The power of holiness

He asked me, 'What do you see?' I answered, 'I see a flying scroll, twenty cubits long and ten cubits wide'… I asked, 'What is it?' He replied, 'It is a basket.' And he added, 'This is the iniquity of the people throughout the land.' (NIV)

Dreams, no matter how weird or confusing, can sometimes reveal how we're feeling; both my husband and I often dream that we're preaching in our pyjamas – a sign of our felt vulnerability! More importantly, God may use dreams and visions, no matter how unusual, to convey messages, just as he did through Joseph preceding the devastating famine (Genesis 37—50). So be encouraged to hear God for yourself through today's reading, even if you are struggling to connect with what may seem utterly bizarre.

Despite prophetic urges to repent of past sins that resulted in Israel's exile, godlessness was evidently rife among the people. No prophet, priest or ruling king could prevent individual behaviour that blatantly disregarded God's holiness, so Zechariah received the next two visions. The scroll represents God's word, which teaches us how to live holy lives to honour and reflect his presence, as well as containing warnings of God's judgment on sin. The basket vision represents the struggle between good (the angels) and evil (the woman trying to escape). Evil is a force to be reckoned with, but the vision assures us of God's faithfulness to remove our sin; a promise fulfilled through Christ.

It is significant that these messages follow on from yesterday's theme of our need for the Holy Spirit to empower God's work through our lives. To experience this greater empowering relies on our yielding to the conviction and prompts that increasingly transform us into uncluttered vessels through which the Holy Spirit may flow.

Each of us must decide if devoting ourselves to pursuing God's holiness is something we desire as an opportunity to experience more of his presence and power. It is certainly something I would like to know and experience more, what about you?

Forgive me, Lord, when I'm apathetic or disinterested in yielding to your holy life. Thank you for the opportunity it offers to know you more and experience your power in greater measure; a gift that truly inspires my devotion. Amen
ANNE LE TISSIER

Diligent participant or dormant observer

'Here is the man whose name is the Branch, and he will branch out from his place and build the temple of the Lord… Those who are far away will come and help to build the temple of the Lord… This will happen if you diligently obey the Lord your God.' (NIV)

There is a lot to consider in this short chapter, so let's dive straight in.

Zechariah's eighth vision of the night repeats the message of the first; God alone controls the events of history; all the earth belongs to him, whether or not its inhabitants acknowledge him. So, for now, let's focus on verses 9–15.

Joshua, the high priest, was not of royal descent, but was crowned to symbolise the one whom he foreshadowed. The Messiah, called 'the Branch', both here and in chapter 3, would 'branch out' from beyond the Jews in Jerusalem to those 'far off' i.e. the Gentiles, to involve them in building the temple. It's another example of Zechariah's visions looking farther ahead than the physical rebuilding in Jerusalem to the future spiritual temple, embracing all nations through the person and work of the Messiah. But a question is left hanging in verse 15: will they be the kind of people who are ready to participate in God's coming kingdom and diligently play their part in being built into a holy temple of the Lord (see Ephesians 2:19–22)?

God appoints and enables each of us to play our part in the dynamic growth of his church. His Spirit equips us to minister to one another and to reach out to the world with his love, truth, power and message of salvation (1 Corinthians 12:7, 11). So let me leave the question raised in Zechariah with each of us. How can we further nurture the gifts of the Holy Spirit and prioritise God's purpose in our lives? Perhaps our responses might inspire resolutions to pursue in the New Year.

Consider the spiritual gifts God has given you, then prayerfully recommit to serving within his church. If you need help knowing what this might look like, ask your minister or a Christian friend to talk and pray this through with you.

ANNE LE TISSIER

Fasts, feasts and faithfulness

'Was it really for me that you fasted? And when you were eating and drinking, were you not just feasting for yourselves?… Administer true justice; show mercy and compassion to one another. Do not oppress the widow or the fatherless, the foreigner or the poor. Do not plot evil against each other.' (NIV)

My home looks rather bland at the moment as I traditionally leave decorating until a week before Christmas. I've no idea why, as I love going into homes already sparkling with lights, smelling of pine and adorned with festivity. This reading prompted my thoughts about traditions, from observing key dates in the Christian calendar to upholding spiritual disciplines, such as fasting.

Almost two years after his night visions, Zechariah responded to a question (vv. 2–3). The exiled Jews had incorporated additional fasts into their religious calendar to lament events surrounding the destruction of Jerusalem. With the rebuilding work almost complete, were they still necessary? Their question remained unanswered by Zechariah but provoked one in response; was their outward observance of religious feasts and fasts truly motivated for and by God's heart (see also 8:16–19)?

Christmas is a pertinent time to consider this ourselves, but also in relation to other traditions or disciplines we uphold. What are our motivations in going to church, for example? Is it simply a routine, a means to meet others, to have our needs met, or also to fulfil our part in serving the body of Christ? What motivates our fasting from food? To have our prayers answered, to lose weight, or to seek God's purposes and rekindle concern for justice, kindness and generosity?

As for those of us who will uphold traditional Christmas feasts, may love and loyalty permeate all our relationships, as we celebrate with loved ones and reach out to those in need with practical, spiritual and emotional support. For as Zechariah reminds us, how we treat others – not least the poor and vulnerable – says more about our faith than the traditions we uphold.

Forgive me, Lord, when I've been more concerned about my own needs being met than for your purposes to be worked out. Inspire and revive my Christmas celebrations with your justice, mercy and hope. Amen

ANNE LE TISSIER

The influence of holiness

**'I will return to Zion and dwell in Jerusalem… the Holy Mountain…
I will save you, and you will be a blessing… people from all languages
and nations will… say, "Let us go with you, because we have heard
that God is with you."' (NIV)**

What captivates you? A stunning sunset? Rosebuds? The ocean? Your child's
face? What beauty mesmerizes you, drawing you to it time and again, holding your interest and attention, inspiring creativity and response, perhaps
even shaping your priorities and how you live?

The Bible speaks of the beauty of God's holiness; holiness being a recurrent theme in Zechariah, and no wonder, as it's a vital element in attracting
others to God. Holy lives are imbued with truth, justice, goodness, honesty
and integrity, avoiding all forms of insincerity or hypocrisy (vv. 16–17) –
much like we read in 7:9–10.

You may be familiar with broader definitions of holiness, such as being
set apart in devotion to God, but I'm also inspired from our reading that
holiness is where the Lord dwells; and where the Lord dwells there is blessing. In fact, ten promised blessings are described in this chapter in relation
to God's holy dwelling; blessings that will attract others to his peace, joy,
provision and productivity.

We have been saved to be and to bring God's blessing to others (v. 13).
Without the hallmark of holiness, however, no one will see the Lord
(Hebrews 12:14). Only God's indwelling presence can make us holy, but
Hebrews urges us to be holy as we yield to his nature; allowing it to shape
us into his image with divine qualities that attract others to want to know
him for themselves.

Perhaps there are times however, when we try to appear holy without
pursuing it at our core. If that resonates in your heart, simply begin by
making space to gaze on the beauty of God's love, truth, character and
promises. As you repeat this over time, he will captivate and inspire you,
and your devoted response will in turn draw others toward him too.

---

*If it's helpful, use this prompt adapted from Psalm 27:4 to pause and gaze
on God: 'One thing I ask of you Lord, that I may dwell in your presence every
moment, to gaze on the beauty of your holiness.'*

ANNE LE TISSIER

Build yourself up in your holy faith

'Rejoice greatly, Daughter Zion! Shout, Daughter Jerusalem! See, your king comes to you, righteous and victorious, lowly and riding on a donkey, on a colt, the foal of a donkey.' (NIV)

I was brought up by an atheist father and a nominally believing mother, but came to faith (with my mum) during my teens. It wasn't long before my newfound beliefs were questioned, argued and dismissed. In fact, there were times I doubted I was right. But these uncertainties urged me to dig deeper; to know the one in whom I believed and the reasons for my beliefs (2 Timothy 1:12; 1 Peter 3:15). And prophecy played a part in that.

Zechariah is called the most messianic of all the Old Testament books. He is the most quoted prophet in the gospel passion narratives (and with Ezekiel, in Revelation). Zechariah declared that the Messiah would come as the Lord's servant, the branch (3:8; 6:12), as both king and priest (6:13) and as the true shepherd (11:4–11). He would be betrayed for 30 pieces of silver (11:12–13), crucified (12:10) and forsaken (13:7), but his dominion would eventually reach the ends of the earth (9:10) concluding with his Second Advent (14:4). Today we're reminded of the messianic prophecy fulfilled 400 years later, when the inhabitants of Jerusalem erupted in praise as Jesus entered its gates, riding on the colt of a donkey (v. 9; Matthew 21:1–11; Mark 11:1–11).

Jude encourages us to build ourselves up in the foundations of our faith (Jude 1:20) and an invaluable way we can do that is to recall messianic prophecies and their fulfilment in Jesus. Their truth instils peace and assurance, shapes a godly outlook and deepens our trust in God. Christmas may offer increased opportunities to share the reasons for what we believe, and these prophecies add weight to our witness. So, let's be ready to talk about our faith and follow that up with prayer; trusting God to water the spiritual seeds we've sown.

Take time, if you are able during this season of Advent and Christmas, to reacquaint yourself with passages that were fulfilled in the coming of Jesus.
ANNE LE TISSIER

Distracted or dependent

Ask the Lord for rain in the springtime… The idols speak deceitfully, diviners see visions that lie; they tell dreams that are false, they give comfort in vain. Therefore the people wander like sheep oppressed for lack of a shepherd. (NIV)

We live in a world filled with opinions, pressures, enticements and coercion, much as the Israelites did in Zechariah's day: a world that offers other ways of looking at or doing life that can lure us away from dependency on God.

To 'ask' reminded Judah that God controlled the source of blessing on their crops, flocks and herds (v. 1), and that his power to provide should not be passively assumed. Zechariah wasn't just referring to physical blessings, he was continuing his theme of salvation (9:16). Rain symbolised their deeper spiritual needs which only God could provide for.

But the shepherds leading God's flock were depending on idols and failing to lead God's people in his truth. Left to drift aimlessly, they were vulnerable to oppression and affliction (v. 2). However, God always looks out for his people and the metaphors used in verses 3–4 symbolised the stability and victory of Christ's leadership on which their destiny hinged.

As priests of the new covenant, we're inspired to keep asking for God's blessing, direction and provision, rather than passively assume it (Matthew 7:7–11). God promises so much, but we can be tempted to resort to seemingly easier or more enticing options for assurance, guidance, self-worth, purpose, security and provision. Being intentional in asking prompts us to keep drawing close in dependent relationship with God, and guards us from seeking out emotional, mental or physical wellbeing in the wrong places.

Relationships, mentors, financial security or benchmarks of success can provide helpful advice, comfort, security, support and fulfilment. However, our primary place of dependency for well-being and influence is in God who will never let us down.

Lord, forgive my distracted heart. You are my source of values, goals, self-worth, productivity, guidance and contentment. I sit with you now, receiving this reassurance. Amen

ANNE LE TISSIER

Bless and pray for those who are against you

So I shepherded the flock marked for slaughter, particularly the oppressed of the flock. Then I took two staffs and called one Favour and the other Union, and I shepherded the flock. In one month I got rid of the three shepherds. The flock detested me. (NIV)

Since my early 20s I've been regularly praying for our government. At times I've prayed for God to raise up godly leaders of faith, assuming that if they were dedicated to the good of the people, ridding the land of injustice and encouraging peace, they would receive a warm welcome. As our reading highlights, however, such rulers may be rejected.

This passage offers a number of potential interpretations, but the key message conveys that Israel will again suffer judgment and desolation when they reject God's good shepherd. Like the shepherd in Psalm 23 he will use two staffs, albeit symbolic, to lead and care for the flock. 'Favour' also known as grace, beauty or kindness, represents qualities of godly leadership and the blessings his people will consequently enjoy. 'Union' from such leadership results in harmonious relationships. But when the people reject him, God will raise up a foolish and worthless shepherd (vv. 15–17); selfish, greedy and corrupt.

The adulation for Jesus, promptly followed by betrayal, rejection and crucifixion, is a poignant reminder that though we are called to reflect God's character and truth, not everyone will like us or accept our belief in Jesus. The scale of rejection spans from brutal oppression to mild disagreement or ridicule, but when it happens, let's focus on the bigger picture: it isn't always us that they dislike or reject, it is Jesus in us (Luke 10:16).

When others shun our lifestyle, character or witness we may feel hurt, embarrassed, isolated or angry. But we are called to love others deeply, to pray for their salvation and to live godly lives so that despite their accusations, some may see God in us and find him for themselves (1 Peter 2:12).

Pray for God's blessing and enlightenment on someone you know who has rejected your faith. How might you love them today? Pray also for Christians suffering persecution: for strength, protection and power in their witness.

ANNE LE TISSIER

Inspired to worship

'And I will pour out… a spirit of grace and supplication. They will look on me, the one they have pierced, and they will mourn for him as one mourns for an only child.' (NIV)

Picture the newborn in the Christmas nativity, exposed to an unhygienic feeding trough and threats on his life from Herod. See the baby grown to a man: no home of his own, walking hundreds of miles in seasonal extremes of heat and rain and exhausted by endless needs of vast crowds. He was resented by religious officials, then despised, rejected and tortured to death. With sheer lavish love, Jesus left his Father's side, becoming nothing in the eyes of the world, to restore eternal union with God and infuse a heavenly inheritance to our earthly existence; something to keep in mind as we ponder our text.

With increasing intensity, Zechariah's final chapters pick up themes from chapters 9—11 as the day of the messianic kingdom approaches and God's justice defeats evil (12:1–9). But the tone changes remarkably from verse 10, for 'that day' is linked to the rejection of the messianic shepherd ('the one they have pierced'). God's people needed a new spirit (v. 10) and a new cleansing (13:1), so God poured out a spirit of grace and supplication; their sin exposed but their subsequent guilt and grief redeemed by love.

It is God's kindness that inspires repentance, not the other way round. I'm sure that you're deeply moved, as I am, by his love, mercy and faithfulness, relieving you of angst, shame and fear. For the prophecy was fulfilled – God's good shepherd came as the baby in Bethlehem to offer life at great cost to himself. If ever there was an invitation to pause from our reflections, it is now. Let's still our thoughts from outstanding jobs to complete before Christmas, focus our hearts on Jesus, and make space to respond with gratitude and worship.

Glory to you, my God, in the highest heaven. All praise to you Jesus, my Saviour. Wondrous Holy Spirit of peace, counsel and comfort, I am so grateful to you. Receive the adoration of my heart.

ANNE LE TISSIER

To be or not to be, a prophet

'On that day every prophet will be ashamed of their prophetic vision. They will not put on a prophet's garment of hair in order to deceive.' (NIV)

Prophets, like Zechariah, brought challenging as well as encouraging words from God; calling the people back to their spiritual roots and teaching them how to apply God's word. But their authority and anointing resulted from first being drastically changed themselves when they responded to God's call.

Our penultimate chapter continues to foretell the rejection of God's gift of a shepherd to his people and the scattering of the flock (vv. 7–8); fulfilled when Christ's disciples deserted him in Gethsemane, and with the dispersion of the Jews in AD70. It also condemns the prophets who spoke falsely in God's name (vv. 2–6). This was an inherent problem before and after the exile. Like Zechariah, Jesus warned against those who appeared to give messages from God yet failed to live in devoted relationship with him. In contrast, those who lived out his teachings proved their devotion and authenticity, and in turn, their anointing (Matthew 7:15–23).

Paul teaches us to receive prophetic messages with an open, respectful heart, but to seek spiritual wisdom to test their source; then we can hold on to what is from God and reject what is not (1 Thessalonians 5:19–20). Part of that testing will come from the prophets themselves; do they live in close, yielded, relationship to God? Does the fruit of their lives – their words, tone, attitudes and behaviour – reflect Christ's?

We can all reflect on that testing if we sense we have a word from the Lord. Are we letting God challenge and change us by those words before we expect it of others? Is the word inspired by God's Spirit or merely something we'd like to happen for the person we share it with?

Lord, I ask for your gift of prophecy so that I may build others up in their faith. Please give me spiritual discernment to hear from you, humility in my response, and confidence to share it with grace and love. Amen

ANNE LE TISSIER

On that day

On that day living water will flow out from Jerusalem… The Lord will be king over the whole earth. On that day there will be one Lord, and his name the only name. (NIV)

Hope is a feeling of desire for something without that outcome being assured. Perhaps you have such hopes for Christmas – or for your life. The meaning of hope in scripture, however, is translated from a word meaning absolute certainty in the outcome. And it's this kind of confident assurance which Zechariah feeds to our hearts, minds and souls.

Zechariah repeatedly refers to the day of the Lord – the end of times as we know them. The language is apocalyptic (highly symbolic and prophetic) as he concludes the book describing events leading up to the establishment of God's kingdom. It is difficult to determine what will take place literally, in the spiritual realm, or what is symbolic, but Acts 1:9–12 confirms the return of the Messiah as prophesied in Zechariah 14:4, when holiness will characterise all of life without distinction between sacred and secular.

Jesus said we would have difficulties in life, but we have the confident hope of Zechariah's prophecies to settle our emotions, shape our thinking and nurture our strength in God. Just knowing about this hope, however, isn't enough. To experience its steadying, sustaining reassurance and outlook, we shift our focus from our difficulties on to our hope in Jesus. To know this hope for ourselves comes from a proactive choice rather than a passive faith; a choice to open our hearts and minds to the presence and power of God's Spirit with us, whenever problems undermine our peace.

This study is finishing but I pray this truth will remain with you. Jesus is with you, and for you, no matter the issues you are facing; he is your true source of life to help you with each day, and to assure you with confidence for your future.

Thank you, Lord, for your presence with me now and forever. I pause to open my mind and heart to the life of your Spirit, but anticipate the day when I will see and experience you fully, face-to-face. Amen

ANNE LE TISSIER

Angels from the realms of glory

Sara Batts-Neale writes:

Hark the heralds, singing in exultation, saying the first Noel, bidding us not to be afraid. As we journey through the last week of Advent into Christmas and the final days of the year, we're going to be looking at the ministry of angels.

What sort of picture springs to mind when you think about angels? I wonder if you first think of children in nativity plays – cardboard wings, tinsel crowns, and full of childhood innocence. My starring role came at the age of eight, on the brink of a chickenpox outbreak! Or perhaps your go-to angel is Clarence, from the film *It's a Wonderful Life*. In this 1946 classic, Clarence is sent to help despairing businessman George Bailey understand exactly what his value is to the community around him. It's required viewing in my house over Christmas for its message of hope, and the reminder of how we can be salt and light in the world – sometimes unknowingly.

However, Clarence – and the beautiful angels we have on our Christmas cards – might tempt us to make them in our image. A slightly holier version of us, perhaps. There are thousands of artworks that present angels as young, flawless and blonde. Yet as we read about angels more carefully, we realise they are far more awesome and far stranger than our Christmas ideas suggest.

We will explore how encounters with angels change lives – and why they so often start their speeches with 'Do not be afraid'. We will look at their appearances in stories that shaped the history of God's people, and in the encounters that shaped the post-resurrection church. We will see angels in hopeful dreams and extraordinary visions. We'll take a diversion to what I think is the funniest story in the Bible. And yes, we will read of the pivotal part angels played in the annunciation and the nativity.

Let us not domesticate these awesome messengers who bring us something of the fear of God and the splendour of his majesty. Let us move beyond the Christmas card and explore the ministry of angels.

Angels in fiery places

There the angel of the Lord appeared to him in a flame of fire out of a bush; he looked, and the bush was blazing, yet it was not consumed. (NRSV)

I love the O Antiphons, which we studied at the beginning of Advent (see page 100). They are a highlight of the year. As many Christians will sing 'O Adonai' today and reflect on this story of Moses' encounter with God in the burning bush, it seems a fitting place to start our study.

So where's the angel in this? It's a small part, perhaps, compared to the angelic appearances yet to come. But the angel is there all right – appearing to Moses 'in a flame of fire out of a bush'. The angel, it seems, provides the flames that set the bush ablaze and grabs Moses' attention. We can see immediately that the idea of angels as depicted on most Christmas cards is already a bit limited, since we don't often see pictures of the burning bush at this time of year.

Angels are God's messengers. They are scene-setters, heralds, pointing past themselves to something bigger. The angel of the Lord literally prepares the ground for God to speak to Moses. The angel doesn't take a human form – and in other places in the Bible angels can't be seen unless God reveals them, as we will see on Tuesday.

The angel in the burning bush heralds God's call to Moses to remember he is on holy ground. The fire makes Moses turn aside from his daily routine. Where is your attention at the moment? With a week to go before Christmas, how is the balance of prayer and preparation? I think it's easy for the 'stuff' of Christmas to distract us. Despite being a period of spiritual preparation, Advent so easily becomes overwhelmed by the pre-Christmas activities. So perhaps today our challenge is to allow our attention to be caught by the appearance of an angel.

O Adonai and ruler of the House of Israel, you appeared to Moses in the fire of the burning bush, and on Mount Sinai gave him your law: Come, and with an outstretched arm redeem us! Amen

SARA BATTS-NEALE

Angels in uncomfortable places

'How awesome is this place! This is none other than the house of God, and this is the gate of heaven.' (NRSV)

Today we read about Jacob's vision at the place he called Bethel. At night he dreamed of the angels of God ascending and descending. God's messengers, coming back and forth, showing how they exist in our realm and in heaven.

Jacob takes a stone for a pillow, which sounds extremely uncomfortable. Perhaps you're the kind of person who can sleep anywhere and at any time. Or maybe sleep has been elusive lately, and nights have become difficult despite a pleasant bed. This made me wonder about the uncomfortable times and places in which we find ourselves from time to time. Yesterday we thought about the busyness of Advent. Yet, this season of preparation for Christmas is not always as joyful and exciting as some may make out. Is it, instead, a time you dread of fraught family relationships, complicated expectations and a distinct lack of peace and goodwill? Recent Christmases have been overshadowed by Covid-19 and I can guess there are many of us living with grief, job loss, uncertainty, illness, the list goes on – and these are all times which are as uncomfortable as a stone pillow. And yet, 'surely the Lord is in this place' (v. 16).

I'm not suggesting we should become superheroes or saints and begin to celebrate difficult times – nor to assume that they only happen because of a lack of faith or as a punishment from God. We all have them. Yet just as Jacob saw angels ascending and descending, touching the earth, we too can be assured that God touches the earth. Jesus is the word made flesh who dwelt among us. God is with us – now, in this very moment.

Lord Jesus, we know you are with us however we are feeling and whatever our circumstances. Thank you for your unfailing love, and for the peace you offer when our souls are troubled. Amen

SARA BATTS-NEALE

Angels in unlikely places

Then the Lord opened the eyes of Balaam, and he saw the angel of the Lord standing in the road. (NRSV)

Yesterday we thought about difficult places. In contrast, today we read what l think is one of the silliest stories in the Bible. Granted, the Bible isn't the first place we look for humour or slapstick, but I just cannot imagine this scene without amusement.

Balaam has been summoned to curse God's people. En route, the angel of the Lord blocks the donkey's way. Balaam can't see the angel – only the donkey can. Picture the scene – the long-suffering donkey trying to get round the angel by going into a field or squeezing along a narrow path. In the end, the donkey gives up and lies down. When the donkey is given the power of speech, it is most indignant at the treatment meted out by Balaam.

So we have the image of a dignified man at the mercy of his donkey. Balaam has no idea what's going on. Once we're past the silliness (and, perhaps, our disquiet at the treatment of a beast of burden), there are serious messages here.

First, the way others see the world may include ideas we're not able to perceive and understand. And second, those we might deem foolish often have wisdom and knowledge to impart. In some of Shakespeare's plays the figure of the fool is the one who speaks the truth of a situation and can do so precisely because they are not held in high regard. I wonder if we have people around us whose words we ignore.

I wonder if, sometimes, when we're so convinced we're right, it's the pratfalls that open our eyes to the reality of our situation. When we're not in control, we might be able to hear and see the messengers God sends. Although it probably won't be via a talking donkey.

Some things in life do demand to be taken seriously. Yet there is room for frivolity, seeing the daft side of things. Laughter is a joyful part of being human. Is there enough light-heartedness in your life?

SARA BATTS-NEALE

Angels in dangerous places

'My God sent his angel and shut the lions' mouths so that they would not hurt me, because I was found blameless before him; and also before you, O king, I have done no wrong.' (NRSV)

Angels appearing to donkeys, and now angels as lion-tamers? This very well-loved Bible story contains a lesson for us about the power of God through his messengers. For me, the challenge of the tales I learned as a child is to see beyond the familiar, and fully understand the awesome strangeness of our God. The book of Daniel is full of visions, battles and heavenly powers, so it is perhaps unsurprising that we should also find angels in its pages. Gabriel himself is mentioned, interpreting one of Daniel's visions (Daniel 8:16–17).

Daniel is thrown into the lions' den because he refused to give up his worship of God. Yet Daniel is extracted, uninjured the following morning – and I see here echoes of the story we will read next week of Peter's release from prison. We know from the book of Revelation, which we will explore next week, that angels are continually worshipping God. And Daniel continued to worship despite scheming presidents and satraps.

We hear what happens to these conspirators, and it's not pretty. These lions were not merely disgruntled pussy cats – but fearsome, hungry beasts. Yet the angel was able to overcome them, shutting their mouths, keeping Daniel safe from harm. A guardian angel? A reward for Daniel's faithfulness? Perhaps. I think there's more here, too. The angel makes a place of danger into a place of safety. The angel does the work of God in an extraordinary place and in an extraordinary way. The angel proves that God has power over everything. We can leave the last word to King Darius, who declares, 'He is the living God, enduring forever. His kingdom shall never be destroyed, and his dominion has no end' (v. 26).

Lord God, your angel showed King Darius your power. Help us to keep our trust in you as Daniel did, that we might show your glory in our lives and in our worship. Amen

SARA BATTS-NEALE

Angels in holy places

Zechariah said to the angel, 'How will I know that this is so? For I am an old man, and my wife is getting on in years.' (NRSV)

One frustrating side effect of getting older is my inability to say the words I want. Asking my husband for a vegetable last week, I ended up calling it the 'one that's white, not broccoli'. So I have sympathy for Zechariah, robbed of all speech. He was trying to explain an angelic visitation, not just ask for cauliflower!

The announcement to Zechariah that his wife will fall pregnant has all the elements we expect in a story about an encounter with an angel: fear, disbelief and life-changing consequences.

Zechariah is in the sanctuary – a place that only priests could go. Everyone else is outside, praying. Gabriel appears, which is understandably terrifying. Gabriel brings the news that Elizabeth will have a child. Not just an ordinary child, but one who will 'make ready a people prepared for the Lord' (v. 17). Zechariah questions this pronouncement. He's not the first to question a pregnancy – this passage echoes the words of Sarah, Abraham's wife, as she is promised a son (Genesis 18). Sarah laughs, is overheard and afraid. Zechariah asks for some kind of proof – after all, he knows that he and Elizabeth are not in their first flush of youth. He gets his sign – he's struck dumb. I wonder how long it took those who were waiting outside for him to realise he'd had a vision?

Zechariah and Elizabeth's lives are changed by this encounter with an angel. Ordinary people are given a part in the story of the coming of the Messiah. Sadness and disgrace are turned into joy. I wonder if Zechariah's silence is genuinely punishment; might loss of speech instead be a gift of silence – silence in which he grows from doubt, to burst forth in a song of prophecy and praise (Luke 1:67–79).

'And you, child, will be called the prophet of the Most High; for you will go before the Lord to prepare his ways, to give knowledge of salvation to his people by the forgiveness of their sins.' (Luke 1:76–77)

SARA BATTS-NEALE

Angels in dream places

An angel of the Lord appeared to him in a dream and said, 'Joseph, son of David, do not be afraid to take Mary as your wife, for the child conceived in her is from the Holy Spirit.' (NRSV)

Today we look at one of the accounts of the birth of Jesus and we begin with Matthew's account.

Some nights we don't remember our dreams. Some mornings we wake up wondering how the convoluted narrative ends. Like many of us, I have a recurrent anxiety dream – when it happens, it's a sign my days need a bit of calming attention.

Joseph has an encounter with an angel after the news of Mary's pregnancy is public. That was probably a pretty stressful time for him. Before he can send her away, an angel appears in his dream and reassures him. I wonder what that dream might have been like? Was it a gentle reassurance or was Joseph afraid? I wonder if Joseph was anxious, too? Matthew tells us he was a righteous man. He did not want to see Mary publicly disgraced. Perhaps the appearance of the angel was a relief to his sense of propriety and justice.

It's a different kind of encounter than Zechariah's – there is no room for doubt, no drama. Just a dream in which Joseph is encouraged in his righteousness – and his life is changed.

Encounters with angels change lives. Encounters with something that is clearly from God ought to! How could we turn our backs on the word of God when it comes from the mouth of his messenger? If only all our guidance from God was so clearly given…

I wonder whether the angelic appearance helped Joseph understand the truth of Mary's story about her encounter with Gabriel. Perhaps Joseph needed to experience an angelic visitation himself to really believe Mary. Perhaps Joseph's dream helped him take his place, with confidence, in God's unfolding story.

O Emmanuel, our king and our lawgiver, the hope of the nations and our Saviour: Come and save us, O Lord our God. Amen

SARA BATTS-NEALE

Angels in virgin places

In the sixth month the angel Gabriel was sent by God to a town in Galilee called Nazareth, to a virgin engaged to a man whose name was Joseph, of the house of David. The virgin's name was Mary. (NRSV)

Today, Christmas Eve, we have what might be the appearance of the angel Gabriel we've been waiting for: Gabriel's words spoken in a thousand nativity plays, the event depicted in a myriad of artworks – the Annunciation itself. Gabriel's words lead to Mary's 'yes' and her taking up her place in God's story of redemption and love.

I wonder how you imagine the scene portrayed today. How does the Mary you visualise behave? Is she a mirror of the representations we have seen in famous artworks – dressed in blue, eyes downcast? I have a rather different poster on my wall – it's Mary as the wartime Rosie the Riveter, the symbol of women in the workforce during World War II. There's no meek submission there to the life-changing news Gabriel brings for Mary! And what does your Gabriel look like? Is he friendly or fearsome?

I love the way Luke describes Mary's reactions. Mary 'pondered what kind of greeting this might be' (v. 29). Clearly not just an ordinary 'hello!' She is curious and reflective. She is perplexed, but not afraid. So I wonder if Gabriel's injunction 'do not be afraid,' might have more to do with the momentous news he is about to impart and less to do with his presence. He doesn't 'appear' as he did to Zechariah – Gabriel's approach to Mary seems much gentler. He also doesn't need to introduce himself, in the same way he did with Zechariah. There's no sense of Mary being startled, for example. So did she immediately recognise Gabriel as an angel? Had she heard already about Zechariah's encounter a few months before? The message Gabriel brings is world changing.

Lord Jesus, your mother Mary was full of grace. We thank you for her life, for her 'yes' to God's messenger and for all that we can learn from her faithfulness. Amen

SARA BATTS-NEALE

Happy Christmas! Happy birthday, Jesus!

And suddenly there was with the angel a multitude of the heavenly host, praising God and saying, 'Glory to God in the highest heaven, and on earth peace among those whom he favours!' (NRSV)

The Christmas angels. The angelic host. The ones whose glory fills the skies. The ones we are so familiar with, returning each December to their images and their message in cards, carols and decorations. There are two things about the angels I'd like to focus on in today's passage.

First, the angel of Lord and the glory of the Lord appear together. Psalm 19 tells us that the 'heavens are telling the glory of God'. Perhaps what happened when the angel appeared was that the shepherds' focus was changed; perhaps the encounter with the angel allowed them to see the glory of God in creation, in detail. Wouldn't that kind of perception be amazing? To see with our eyes and our heart what it really means for God to be present, creating, sustaining? I suspect it would also be part of the terror that the shepherds experience – and so the angel gives that now-familiar reminder, 'Do not be afraid'.

The second thing to note is that we have not just one angel and the glory of the Lord to contend with but also a multitude of the heavenly host. They praise God. And that's enough for today, Christmas Day, the day we celebrate the birth of the child wrapped in cloth and lying in a manger. The day we celebrate God incarnate; God in his creation, the fully human and fully divine first day of Jesus. It is a terrific concept to grasp – the glory of God, creator of the universe, as a tiny human baby. Can you take a moment now to reflect on how awesome it is that God is in this place?

Happy Christmas!

'Joyful, all ye nations rise, join the triumph of the skies, with th' angelic host proclaim, "Christ is born in Bethlehem".'

SARA BATTS-NEALE

Noticing angels

The angel of the Lord found her by a spring of water in the wilderness, the spring on the way to Shur. And he said, 'Hagar, slave-girl of Sarai, where have you come from and where are you going?' (NRSV)

Today, Boxing Day, has traditionally been associated with generosity. One day a year where the rich would notice the existence of the poor, perhaps, as they packed up charity gifts. Our verses today echo the idea of being noticed – and how the angel of the Lord notices a mere slave, Hagar.

The angel of the Lord appeared to her twice as she plays out her role in the history of God's people, reminding us that the marginalised are not forgotten.

Notice the first thing the angel says. He names Hagar. He uses her name. She is seen. She is identified. Our names and our identities are so important. Hagar's treatment at Sarah's hands was enough to remove her sense of self – here it is regained. In many ways this is a tricky Bible story to engage with. The casual mistreatment of Hagar shines a challenging light on to the ways that our Bible is full of stories of slaves and their owners. It shows us a very different culture – one where Hagar being a slave isn't questioned at all. And the angel's bidding to return home and expect trouble is hardly heartening. Hagar heads back to the mistreatment, ultimately only to be cast out into the desert about 13 years later. That feels wrong to our sense of justice.

What this story and the angel's ministry reinforced for me is that God really does know us all regardless of our status or our sense of holiness and worth. We are all known by name; we are all valuable and we are all loved. That's the message I preach most often, alongside that the gift of attention we can give to someone else is priceless.

God, help us to see others as you do. Help us to notice those who live on the margins and show them your love. Amen

SARA BATTS-NEALE

Disconcerting cherubim

In the middle of it was something like four living creatures… The living creatures darted to and fro, like a flash of lightning. (NRSV)

'Please inform your GP if you notice anything unusual,' says the information leaflet in a pack of tablets. Well, I thought, I just saw my dog refuse a biscuit, does that count? Sometimes it's hard for me not to read the literal meaning, even when I know that's not what was intended. I need to see beyond the words to the ideas presented. And that's true of this reading – with some very unusual creatures appearing.

Ezekiel 10 identifies them as cherubim and they are certainly very different from the chubby cherubim we might see on our Christmas cards. There really is something beyond our human grasp, beyond our language of description, that we miss if we create angels in our own image.

If we domesticate our angels, if we keep them cute and understandable, we are missing something of the glory of God. Angels are not created in the image of humans, after all. Ezekiel's vision gives us a prompt to really stretch our theological imaginations to appreciate something of the strange and overwhelming nature of angels.

Angels are more than just kind messengers. They point to the unknowable mystery that is our God. They point to his incomprehensible awesomeness and his true status as creator, majesty and king. They help us embrace the unimaginable, which means we are getting close to God. These angels don't deliver a life-changing message in words the way Gabriel does. Their ministry comes from their reflection of the glory of God. Their message to us is that God is unfathomably awesome.

The idea of God ought to be overwhelming – because if it isn't, if God is something we think we can capture and understand, then it isn't God, to paraphrase St Augustine.

SARA BATTS-NEALE

Obedient angels

Bless the Lord, O you his angels, you mighty ones who do his bidding, obedient to his spoken word. (NRSV)

I'm the kind of person who likes to know what I've got to do, when, and with whom. Ministry life doesn't often allow for such predictability. Perhaps that is why I am drawn to Psalm 103 with its clear description of what angels do. They do God's bidding and are obedient to his word. Job done!

However, I know that this simplicity of purpose is a lot easier for angels than mere mortals. These verses from Psalm 103 might be familiar to you from funeral services – words that remind us of our human frailty. We are but dust – formed by God. He loves us, forgives us and has compassion towards us. These words are of great comfort at times of grief, and in happier days.

This psalm helps us understand ourselves a bit better, and it helps us understand angels a bit better. It helps put our relationship with God in perspective – showing us what we have to be thankful for and how immense his love is.

Listening to God's word, being obedient to him, doing his will – these are all things angels do that we can try to do, too. We're off to a good start by engaging with these notes, helping us reflect on God's word and what it means for us. Obedience – now that's a bit trickier for me. I hope I am obedient – but I also know I am human, stubborn, and as likely to find ways to decide my actions by myself as I am to stop and pray for guidance. I'm definitely not an angel! That makes it even more comforting to read Psalm 103 and know that I'm loved, and God understands I am, after all, a mere human being.

Heavenly Father, we thank you for the example that angels give us. Help us to praise you as they do and to listen to your word as they do. Amen

SARA BATTS-NEALE

Fearsome angels

And suddenly there was a great earthquake; for an angel of the Lord, descending from heaven, came and rolled back the stone and sat on it. (NRSV)

Wivenhoe, where I live, makes much of its history as a fishing port. We also tell the story of the damage wrought by the 1884 Essex earthquake. I've never been in an earthquake – have you? The aftermath must be as terrifying as the quake itself – wondering if buildings are safe, and accounting for all our loved ones. Mary and Mary Magdalene, at first light, near Jesus' tomb, must have been terrified. Yet they were able to face the angel – without fainting, like the guards did. That's a detail that we women need to notice – the guards faint, but the women are strong and able to face the fear. A reversal of all those feminine stereotypes! I suppose they have already had the worst happen, haven't they? Their beloved Jesus has been killed. What else would be able to touch them in their moment of raw grief?

The angel has a clear and unequivocal message for the women. He tells them to see for themselves that Jesus is no longer there, and to go tell the disciples that Jesus will see them in Galilee.

Unlike Zechariah or Mary, mother of Jesus, Mary Magdalene and the other Mary do not question the angel – they simply do his bidding, carrying with them a mixture of fear and joy.

Here, we see the angel as messenger. I wonder why there is just one who brings the startling news of Jesus' resurrection? It's a contrast to the whole heavenly host who announce his birth. Perhaps only one was needed because God knew these women were faithful and would listen – they knew Jesus, they had begun to understand who he was. That's quite different from the bewildered shepherds 33 or so years earlier, who may have needed more persuasion that something cosmically important was happening!

The angel shares the good news of Jesus' resurrection, modelling for us a clear, precise way to share this ourselves: see the evidence of transformation, know that Jesus will go ahead and meet you, do not be afraid.

SARA BATTS-NEALE

Worshipping angels

Day and night without ceasing they sing, 'Holy, holy, holy, the Lord God the Almighty, who was and is and is to come.' (NRSV)

The ox, lion, eagle and human face, the wheels and the eyes – sound familiar? I think we have another vision of heaven and another vision of the living creatures Ezekiel described which we looked at on Tuesday. Today, they're showing us what worship of God looks like, in the attempt to describe what heaven might be. Notice where John says things are 'like' something else – he can't quite describe the vision he saw, so he has to be approximate.

Revelation is a tricky book – and one I happily ignored for several years on the basis it was too hard to understand. I'd read enough theories of this or that to be thoroughly put off from wading through the weird narrative. Yes, there are lots of strange visions, and yes, there are lampstands. I know I've written before about how 'lampstand' conjures up for me something out of a 1970s sitting room, which somewhat dents the image of glory that runs through the chapters! On a grand scale, however, Revelation shows us quite how extraordinarily different heaven, angels and the worship of God is from the ways we understand it.

Angels worship God without ceasing. God is holy. He is Almighty. He was – from before the beginning of time. He is – with us now. He is to come – in glory, when we will see him face-to-face, and there will be no more tears or sadness (Revelation 21:4). There is no direct message from the heavenly beings to us, but this verse helps us focus on who God is, and how awesome he is. The angels help us to remember that God is our creator, not our creation. He is bigger, stranger and more than we can really imagine.

You are worthy, our Lord and God, to receive glory and honour and power, for you created all things, and by your will they existed and were created. (Revelation 4:11)

SARA BATTS-NEALE

Liberating angels

Peter went out and followed him; he did not realise that what was happening with the angel's help was real; he thought he was seeing a vision. (NRSV)

I'm not much of a New Year's Eve kind of partygoer these days – I don't like being up late and prefer facing 1 January full of energy! Thinking about being 'at the gate of the new year' called to mind Rhoda's excitement in Acts 12.

There's much to be joyous about in the angelic appearance to Peter (unless you are a prison guard or Herod). I love the humanity of Rhoda, so thrilled by Peter's voice that she rushes off, leaving him standing outside at the gate. Just like the women bringing news of Jesus' resurrection (Luke 24:11), the others don't believe her at first.

This passage is full of people not really believing what is going on. Peter is woken, unchained and led out of prison by the angel of the Lord: he thought it was a vision. The angel gives Peter very clear instructions: wake up, get up, get dressed, follow me. As we've seen, angels on a mission generally don't waste their words and expect to be obeyed.

In verse 5, we're told that the church prayed fervently for Peter. They'd seen what happened to James, they knew Herod was powerful – they probably didn't think Peter's imprisonment was going to end well.

For Peter, the angel's instructions set him physically free from an actual prison. I wonder if any of us crave freedom from situations in which we feel trapped. I pray that you might be led into this new year with the confidence and resolve to follow where God leads you.

What will you resolve to change, stop or keep next year in your life of faith? If you make New Year's resolutions, ask God for his guidance and peace as you look to the future.

SARA BATTS-NEALE

BRF Centenary Prayer

Gracious God,
We rejoice in this centenary year
that you have grown BRF
from a local network of Bible readers
into a worldwide family of ministries.
Thank you for your faithfulness
in nurturing small beginnings
into surprising blessings.
We rejoice that, from the youngest to the oldest,
so many have encountered your word
and grown as disciples of Christ.
Keep us humble in your service,
ambitious for your glory
and open to new opportunities.
For your name's sake
Amen

Enabling all ages to grow in faith

Anna Chaplaincy

Living Faith

Messy Church

Parenting for Faith

100 years of BRF

2022 is BRF's 100th anniversary! Look out for details of our special new centenary resources, a beautiful centenary rose and an online thanksgiving service that we hope you'll attend. This centenary year we're focusing on sharing the story of BRF, the story of the Bible – and we hope you'll share your stories of faith with us too.

Find out more at **brf.org.uk/centenary**.

To find out more about our work, visit

brf.org.uk

Sharing
the Story
since 1922

Sharing the Christmas Story
From reading to living the gospel
Sally Welch
978 1 80039 106 2 £8.99

Through each week of Advent, a different aspect of the Christmas story is examined. Within each week, the days are focused on the ways in which the Christmas story is shared. Each day offers a Bible passage, followed by a reflection, questions and a prayer. Suggestions for group study and creative prayer activities are also included.

Centenary Classics:
Companions on the Bethlehem Road
Daily readings and reflections for the Advent journey
Rachel Boulding
978 1 80039 088 1 £14.99 hardback

This book of daily Bible readings and reflections for Advent and Christmas is based around spiritual insights gleaned from some of the best-loved poets of the past. As we travel the road to Christmas in the company of these great poets, we will find our minds enlarged and our hearts touched with something of the wonder and joy of this special season.

The BRF Book of 100 Prayers
Resourcing your spiritual journey
Martyn Payne
978 1 80039 147 5 £12.99 hardback

An illustrated collection of prayers by Martyn Payne. Prayer is at the heart of BRF's work, and this special illustrated anniversary collection is a celebration of prayer for BRF's centenary year. It can be used in a range of different settings. Including sections on prayers of preparation, seasonal prayers, and themed prayers for special times and hard times, it is the daily perfect companion to resource your spiritual journey.

brfonline.org.uk

To order

Online: **brfonline.org.uk**
Telephone: +44 (0)1865 319700
Mon–Fri 9.30–17.00

Delivery times within the UK are normally 15 working days. Prices are correct at the time of going to press but may change without prior notice.

Title	Price	Qty	Total
Sharing the Christmas Story	£8.99		
Companions on the Bethlehem Road	£14.99		
The BRF Book of 100 Prayers	£12.99		

POSTAGE AND PACKING CHARGES			
Order value	UK	Europe	Rest of world
Under £7.00	£2.00	Available on request	Available on request
£7.00–£29.99	£3.00		
£30.00 and over	FREE		

Total value of books	
Donation	
Postage and packing	
Total for this order	

Please complete in BLOCK CAPITALS

Title .... First name/initials .... Surname...

Address..

.... Postcode ....

Acc. No. .... Telephone ....

Email..

Method of payment

☐ Cheque (made payable to BRF)   ☐ MasterCard / Visa

Card no. ⬜⬜⬜⬜ ⬜⬜⬜⬜ ⬜⬜⬜⬜ ⬜⬜⬜⬜

Expires end ⬜M⬜M ⬜Y⬜Y   Security code ⬜⬜⬜   Last 3 digits on the reverse of the card

We will use your personal data to process this order. From time to time we may send you information about the work of BRF. Please contact us if you wish to discuss your mailing preferences **brf.org.uk/privacy**

Please return this form to:

BRF, 15 The Chambers, Vineyard, Abingdon OX14 3FE | **enquiries@brf.org.uk**

For terms and cancellation information, please visit **brfonline.org.uk/terms**.

Each issue of *Day by Day with God* is available from Christian bookshops everywhere. Copies may also be available through your church book agent or from the person who distributes Bible reading notes in your church.

Alternatively you may obtain *Day by Day with God* on subscription direct from the publishers. There are two kinds of subscription:

Individual subscriptions
covering 3 issues for 4 copies or less, payable in advance (including postage & packing).

To order, please complete the details on page 144 and return with the appropriate payment to: BRF, 15 The Chambers, Vineyard, Abingdon OX14 3FE

You can also use the form on page 144 to order a gift subscription for a friend.

Group subscriptions
covering 3 issues for 5 copies or more, sent to one UK address (post free).

Please note that the annual billing period for group subscriptions runs from 1 May to 30 April.

To order, please complete the details on page 143 and return with the appropriate payment to: BRF, 15 The Chambers, Vineyard, Abingdon OX14 3FE

You will receive an invoice with the first issue of notes.

All our Bible reading notes can be ordered online by visiting
brfonline.org.uk/collections/subscriptions

Day by Day with God is also available as
an app for Android, iPhone and iPad
brfonline.org.uk/collections/apps

Follow us on Instagram: **@daybydaywithgod**

All subscription enquiries should be directed to:
BRF, 15 The Chambers, Vineyard, Abingdon OX14 3FE
+44 (0)1865 319700 | **enquiries@brf.org.uk**

DBDWG0322

> All our Bible reading notes can be ordered online by visiting
> **brfonline.org.uk/collections/subscriptions**

The group subscription rate for *Day by Day with God* will be £14.55 per person until April 2023.

☐ I would like to take out a group subscription for _____ (quantity) copies.

☐ Please start my order with the January 2023 / May 2023 / September 2023* issue. I would like to pay annually/receive an invoice* with each edition of the notes. (*delete as appropriate)

Please do not send any money with your order. Send your order to BRF and we will send you an invoice.

Name and address of the person organising the group subscription:

Title _____ First name/initials _____ Surname _____

Address_____

_____ Postcode _____

Telephone _____ Email _____

Church_____

Name and address of the person paying the invoice if the invoice needs to be sent directly to them:

Title _____ First name/initials _____ Surname _____

Address_____

_____ Postcode _____

Telephone _____ Email _____

We will use your personal data to process this order. From time to time we may send you information about the work of BRF. Please contact us if you wish to discuss your mailing preferences **brf.org.uk/privacy**

Please return this form to:
BRF, 15 The Chambers, Vineyard, Abingdon OX14 3FE | **enquiries@brf.org.uk**

For terms and cancellation information, please visit **brfonline.org.uk/terms**.

Bible Reading Fellowship is a charity (233280) and company limited by guarantee (301324), registered in England and Wales

To order online, please visit **brfonline.org.uk/collections/subscription**

☐ I would like to give a gift subscription (please provide both names and addresses)

☐ I would like to take out a subscription myself (complete your name and address details only once)

Title _____ First name/initials _____ Surname _____

Address _____

_____ Postcode _____

Telephone _____ Email _____

Gift subscription name _____

Gift subscription address _____

_____ Postcode _____

Gift subscription (20 words max. or include your own gift card):

_____

_____

Please send *Day by Day with God* beginning with the January 2023 / May 2023 / September 2023 issue (*delete as appropriate*):

(please tick box)	UK	Europe	Rest of world
1-year subscription	☐ £18.30	☐ £26.25	☐ £30.15
2-year subscription	☐ £35.70	N/A	N/A

Optional donation to support the work of BRF £ _____

Total enclosed £ _____ (cheques should be made payable to 'BRF')

Please charge my MasterCard / Visa with £ _____

Card no. ☐☐☐☐ ☐☐☐☐ ☐☐☐☐ ☐☐☐☐

Expires end ☐M☐M ☐Y☐Y   Security code ☐☐☐   Last 3 digits on the reverse of the card

We will use your personal data to process this order. From time to time we may send you information about the work of BRF. Please contact us if you wish to discuss your mailing preferences **brf.org.uk/privacy**

Please return this form to:
BRF, 15 The Chambers, Vineyard, Abingdon OX14 3FE | **enquiries@brf.org.uk**

For terms and cancellation information, please visit **brfonline.org.uk/terms**.

Bible Reading Fellowship is a charity (233280) and company limited by guarantee (301324), registered in England and Wales

DBDWG0322